Kitchen Favorites

The Stumreiter Family Cookbook

Rita E. Westphal
and
Mary Jo Stumreiter Nickum
Editors

PTP
PTP Book Division
Path to Publication Group, Inc.
Arizona

Copyright © 2019
Printed in the United States of America All Rights Reserved

No part of this book may be used or reproduced by any means, graphic, electronic, or mechanical, including photocopying, recording, taping or by any information storage retrieval system without the written permission of the publisher except in the case of brief quotations embodied in articles and reviews.

Reviewers may quote passages for use in periodicals, newspapers, or broadcasts provided credit is given to *The Stumreiter Family Cookbook* by Rita E. Westphal and Mary Jo Stumreiter Nickum and PTP Book Division, Path to Publication Group, Inc.

PTP Book Division
Path to Publication Group, Inc.
16845 E. Avenue of the Fountains #325
Fountain Hills, AZ 85268
www.pathtopublication.net

ISBN: 9781091198395
Library of Congress Cataloging Number
LCCN: 2019937699
Printed in the United States of America
First Edition

DEDICATION

To our family ancestors

Acknowledgments

Thank you to each family member who took the time to share their favorite recipes, and to all those who shared their special talents to make this project possible.

A special thank you to Rita Westphal for the sketches of Kitchen Kitty and to Sabrina Stummreiter-Krause and Stefan Stumreiter for their excellent language translation skills.

Foreword

The German language has a very expressive word, "Gemutlichkeit." In English, it means not only the hearty foods that are served, but also the feelings of friendliness and belonging that gathers everyone together.

This cookbook is a combined collection of our German and American Stumreiter family recipes, some traditional, some contemporary. It is a fitting tribute to our Bavarian roots and our thirty-year anniversary of reuniting our family after a separation of nearly one hundred years. What better way to establish family bonds than to celebrate around the family table feasting on homemade, savory and comforting dishes, some made from recipes passed down through generations.

The recipes in this book are simply delicious, yet they have a complex blend of flavors that really entice you to make them again and again. And, don't forget to add a "pinch" of yourself to each recipe whether it is an altering of an ingredient or your personal presentation of each dish. Make it your own and enjoy!

From our family to yours, Guten Appetit!

The Stumreiter Family

Table of Contents

Main Dishes — 11
Beef
- Hearty Mincemeat Pie — 12
- Mama's Minced Meat Pan — 13
- Old-Time Beef Stew — 14
- "K"s Lunch Wagon Sloppy Joes — 15
- Beef Fillet with Apple and Cheese Crust — 16
- Mama's Pot Roast — 16
- Lillian's Sloppy Joes — 17
- Potato Casserole — 17
- Spaghetti Dinner — 18
- Sabrina's Favorite Beef Roulades with Mashed Potatoes — 19
- Tangy Roast Beef Sandwiches — 21
- Beef Stew with Red Wine — 22
- Venison (Mexican) Meatloaf — 25

Pork
- Harvest Casserole with Wild Rice — 27
- Sweet-Sour Pork — 28
- Tortellini for Dating (otherwise known as "the man getting meal") — 29

Seafood
- Mediterranean Seafood Stew — 30
- Stir Fried Shrimp with Vegetables — 31
- Best-Ever Crab Cakes — 32

Fowl
- Southwestern Turkey Burgers — 33
- Zucchini Hot Dish — 34

Soups
- Sweet Potato and Carrot Soup — 35
- Chili — 36
- Zesty Minestrone Soup — 37

Vegetarian Chili 38
Tortilla Soup 39
Five-Alarm Chili 40

Side Dishes **42**
Cucumbers with Sour Cream 43
Aunt Catherine's Lime Gelatin Salad 44
Grandma's "Reiberdatschi" 44
Rainbow Jello Salad 45
Marinated Vegetable Salad 46
Favorite Coleslaw 47
Kaiserschmarrn 48
Irish White Potatoes: Something out
    Of Nothing 49
Apple-Cabbage Slaw 51
Tomato Salad - Greek Village Style 52
Lillian's Three Bean Salad 54
Boletus Mushrooms in Cream Sauce with
    Pretzel Dumplings 55
Upper Palatinate Bread Dumplings with
    Mushroom Cream Sauce 56
Brown Rice: Easy and Consistently Perfect 58
Taco Salad 60

Bread **61**
Aunt Catherine's Bread Biscuits 62
Cajun Hot Tomato Bread 63
Djanet's Glazed Eggnog Monkey Bread 64
Mama Irene Griffin Stumreiter Hinke's
    White Bread 65

Desserts **66**
Whiskey Pecan Cake 67
Spud and Spice Cake 68
Banana Nut Bread 69
Danish Pastry Apple Bars 70
Mom's Date Filled Sugar Cookies 71

Old-Fashioned Oatmeal Cookies	72
Rhubarb Cake with Streusel Topping	73
Chocolate Chip Date Cake	74
Mama's Molasses Cookies	74
Sour Cream Pear Coffee Cake	75
Large Pearl Tapioca Pudding	76
Cowboy Cookies	77
Fresh Plum Cake (Zwetschgendatschi)	78
Chip's Zucchini Bread	79
German Buttermilk Sheet Cake	80
Lillian's Favorite Christmas Cookie – Date Ball Cookies	81
Lillian's Fruit Bowl Supreme	82
Lillian's Oatmeal Chocolate Chip Cookies	82
Lillian's Poppy Seed Cake	83
Strawberry Gelatin Pretzel Dessert	84

Miscellaneous — **85**

Bill's Plum Liqueur	86
Best Pie Crust	86
Cranberry Celery Seed Salad Dressing	87
Bavarian Obatzda (cheese spread)	88
Brown Rice Pancakes	89
Microwave Nut Brittle	91
Outrageous Granola	92
Citrus Habanero Glaze	93
Grandma's Potato Pancakes with Apple Compote	94

Addendum

Wild Rice Hot Dish	156
Catherine Stumreiter Mabie's Rhubarb Jam	157
Gelatin-Carrot-Pineapple Salad	158
Ryan's Special Brownies	159

Main Dishes

Hearty Mincemeat Pie

3 cups cooked beef or venison stew meat, ground in food processor
3 apples thinly sliced
1 cup raisins
½ cup brown sugar
3 Tablespoons vinegar
Beef juices use to moisten filling

Mix the above ingredients and heat well.
Add to the above mixture:
½ teaspoon salt
¼ teaspoon pepper
½ teaspoon mace
½ teaspoon allspice
1 teaspoon cinnamon
½ teaspoon nutmeg
½ teaspoon cloves

Mix all together and heat through. Put in unbaked pie shell, add top crust and pinch edges tightly closed. Bake at 425 degrees for 30 to 40 minutes.
NOTE: This pie is very good using wild game meats

R. E. Westphal

Mama's Minced Meat Pan

40g fat
400g minced meat
3 large onions
2 or 3 whole paprika
peeled tomatoes
1 cup of rice
3 cups of water
Salt to taste
1 garlic clove
herbs of your choice

Finely chop the onions and fry in hot fat until smooth, then add the meat and fry with constant turning. Then add the cleaned, cut vegetables. Add 1 cup of rice, sauté everything, pour water, season and cover, cook for about 20 minutes. NOTE: Whole paprika can be purchased online or in some specialty food stores.

Katharina Stumreiter

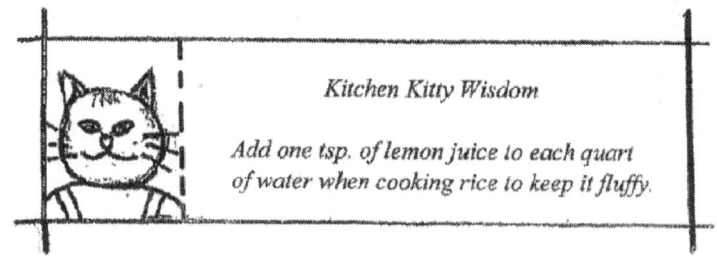

Kitchen Kitty Wisdom

Add one tsp. of lemon juice to each quart of water when cooking rice to keep it fluffy.

Old-Time Beef Stew

1 pound beef chuck, cut in 1-1/2 inch cubes
½ tsp. Worcestershire sauce
½ clove garlic
½ medium onion, sliced
1 bay leaf
½ tbsp. salt
½ tsp. sugar
1/4 tsp. paprika
1/8 tsp. pepper
Dash of ground allspice or cloves
3 carrots pared and quartered
2 potatoes pared and quartered
May add other vegetables to your taste

In Dutch oven, thoroughly brown meat in 1 tbsp of shortening, turning often.
Add 1 cup of beer and rest of ingredients <u>except</u> vegetables. Cover; simmer for 1-1/2 hours, stirring occasionally to keep from sticking. Remove bay leaf and garlic. Add vegetables. Cover and cook 30 to 45 minutes, or till vegetables are tender.

For Gravy: Skim most of fat from liquid; measure 1 cup of liquid. Combine ¼ cup water and 1 tbsp all purpose flour till smooth. Stir slowly into hot liquid. Cook and stir till bubbly. Cook and stir 3 minutes. Serve stew in bowls.

Bill Westphal

"K"s Lunch Wagon Sloppy Joes

2 pounds hamburger cooked and drained of fat
1-10 oz. can tomato soup
¾ cup catsup
¾ cup chopped and cooked celery
¾ cup chopped fresh onion
½ tbsp. Salt
¼ tbsp. Pepper
2 tbsp. Worcestershire sauce
¼ tbsp. Chili powder
¼ tbsp. dry mustard
¼ tbsp. paprika
1 tbsp. brown sugar
1 tbsp. lemon juice
1 tbsp. vinegar

Combine all ingredients and simmer for 20 minutes.

Kareen Mabie England

Catherine with Kareen and Sherburn

Beef Fillet with Apple and Cheese Crust

6 slices of beef tenderloin
salt and pepper
Fat for frying
1 apple
200g Emmentaler cheese
½ c sour cream
1 egg yolk

Season the fillet a bit with salt and pepper and fry in hot fat until the desired cooking point is reached. Peel and grate apple, grate cheese. Mix apple and cheese with egg yolks and sour cream. Spread the fillet with the resulting combination and broil in the oven over high heat.

Silvia Stumreiter

Mama's Pot Roast

1) Brown 3-5 lbs. of Chuck Roast
2) Place in covered roaster pan for 4 hrs. at 325 degrees with 1 cup water and 1 bay leaf
3) At last hour of cooking, add veggies (potato, carrot, rutabaga, celery etc.), add water if needed.

Margo Hinke

Lillian's Sloppy Joes

1 pound ground beef
1-1/2 cups chopped onion
1-1/2 cups chopped celery
1 can tomato soup, condensed
½ cup ketchup
1 tsp. salt
5-6 Hamburger Buns

Brown ground beef. Add onion and celery. Cook until tender but not brown. Add soup, ketchup and salt. Simmer uncovered about 20 minutes or until consistency desired.

Nancy Stumreiter Zappen

Potato Casserole

Brown:
1 pound hamburger
½ cup chopped onion

ADD:
1 can mushroom
½ can tomato soup
3 cups diced potatoes
2 cups diced celery
salt and pepper to taste
Bake at 375 degrees F. for 1 ½ hours.

Kareen Mabie England

Spaghetti Dinner

Sauce:
1 lb. Hamburger (browned and drained)
2 10oz. can tomato paste
2 15oz. can tomato sauce
1 11oz. can tomato soup
1 Tbsp. garlic
¼ tsp. Tabasco sauce
1 Tbsp. Worchester sauce
½ tsp. oregano
½ tsp. basil
1 Tbsp. brown sugar
¼ tsp. crushed red pepper leaves
½ tsp. Italian seasoning

Additional Items Needed:
1 lb. Spaghetti noodles
1 loaf French bread

Mix together and bring to heat level where it bubbles up. Turn down to a simmer. Serve over cooked spaghetti noodles with French bread.

Jonathan and Brandon Hinke (Grandsons of Irene Stumreiter Griffin Hinke)

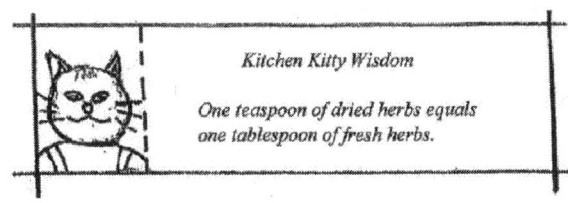

Kitchen Kitty Wisdom

One teaspoon of dried herbs equals one tablespoon of fresh herbs.

Sabrina's Favorite Beef Roulades with Mashed Potatoes

6 beef roulades (thin sliced beef steaks)
1 small jar of pickles
1 small bag of bacon bits
3 – 4 oz. medium-strength mustard
1 bunch of mirepoix (carrot, celery, leek)
2 medium-sized onions
3 -4 oz. tomato paste
1 cup cooking cream
salt
pepper
olive oil
red wine
water
butterfat

For mashed potatoes:

2.2 lbs. potatoes
1 cup milk
2 tbs. butter
salt
nutmeg

Wash and dab the meat, spice with salt and pepper and spread with mustard. Chop up pickles and 1 onion as small as you can and spread on roulades. Spread bacon bits on roulades as well. Roll them up and fix them with toothpicks.
Sear in a casserole with butterfat, then remove from casserole. Coarsely chop the mirepoix, fry well in the remaining butterfat and add a bit of tomato paste. Put

roulades back into casserole and fill up with water and wine until roulades are covered with three-quarters of

liquid. Put casserole with lid into pre-heated oven and braise for 2 hours at 350 degrees F. If necessary, refill with water and wine.
Subsequently, take roulades out of the casserole. Add cooking cream to the liquid and purée for an excellent sauce.
For mashed potatoes: Peel and wash potatoes. Cut into large pieces. Cook in salted water for 20 – 25 min. Strain off water. Put cooking pot back onto warm stove, cover and let remaining water evaporate until the potatoes are dry. Add milk and butter slowly and mash with potato masher. Stir over low heat until creamy. Season with salt and nutmeg.

S. Stummreiter

Eleonora and Fritz Stummreiter

Tangy Roast Beef Sandwiches

1 boneless beef chuck roast (1 Pound)
1 cup water
¼ cup chopped onion
¼ cup chopped celery
1 tablespoon butter
1/3 cup ketchup
3 tablespoons lemon juice
1 tablespoon brown sugar
2 teaspoons red wine vinegar
1 ½ teaspoons Worcestershire sauce
1/8 teaspoon salt
1/8 teaspoon pepper
3 sandwich buns split

Place the roast in a 1 ½ quart slow cooker; add water. Cover and cook on high for 3 hours or until meat is tender. Remove roast; set aside 1/3 cup cooking juices. Shred meat with two forks and return to the slow cooker.
In a small skillet, saute onion and celery in butter. Stir in the ketchup, lemon juice, brown sugar, vinegar, Worcestershire sauce, salt, pepper and reserved cooking juices. Add to slow cooker. Cook on low for 2-3 hours or until heated through and flavors are blended. Serve on buns. Makes 3 servings.

R. E. Westphal

Beef Stew with Red wine

You'll see a ton of recipes out there for French Beef Stew (Boeuf Bourguignon). Many are super complex, but this one is simple enough to give you lots of time to clean up the house before your guests arrive for dinner. As with most soups and stews, this tastes even better the next day! This recipe is inspired by Anthony Bourdain, who I was a massive fan of ever since I read the very first chapter of his book, *Kitchen Confidential*, way back when.

Notice that there is only a little flour used as a thickener. The onions themselves will cook down and become the base of the wonderful gravy-like sauce that coats the meat and carrots. Don't be afraid to break out a ruler to cut the beef, you really do want bite size (but not too small) chunks of meat. The other key to this dish is how you brown the beef. The flavor from browning is the basis of the entire dish – if you screw it up, start over! The first few times I made this dish I didn't brown the beef sufficiently – the result was good, but not great!

One other note...for God's sake do not use the salty, crappy tasteless broth that comes in a cardboard box (heaven forbid bouillon cubes). Buy some high quality frozen stock. Demi-glace is a concentrated sauce, typically made with a meat stock and sometimes wine; it is available on the soup aisle of large grocery stores. If you can't find good stock, just use water!

Ingredients.
3 pounds boneless beef shoulder or neck (chuck), cut into 1 ½-inch pieces
Kosher salt
Freshly ground black pepper

¼ cup canola oil, refined for high heat
4 medium white onions, thinly sliced
2 tablespoons flour
2 cups red burgundy wine (Pinot Noir)
6 medium carrots, cut into 1-inch pieces
2 cloves garlic (whole)
1 bouquet garni (a tied bundle of herbs, typically thyme, bay and parsley)
Beef or Veal stock (or Water if you have no good stock)
Demi-glace (if you can get it)
¼ cup chopped flat-leaf parsley

Equipment:
1 Stock Pot/Roasting Pan or (preferred) Dutch Oven
Ladle/Spoon
Long handled Tongs
Long handled Wooden Spoon
Chopping board and sharp chef knife
2 Large mixing bowls
Cheese Cloth & Kitchen String

Season the meat well with salt and pepper.

Heat the oil your Pot or Dutch Oven over high heat. As soon as the oil shimmers, add the meat in batches and sear on all sides until it is well browned (not gray). If you dump too much meat in the pot at the same time, you'll overcrowd it; cool the thing down and you won't get
good color. Sear the meat a little at a time, transferring it to a plate as it finishes. Be sure to use a long handled wooden spoon or tongs to avoid the hot oil splatters. Towards the final batch, you may need a bit more oil, be sure it heats up properly before adding more of the cubed beef.

When all the meat is done, add the onions to the pot. Reduce the heat to medium-high; cook for about 10 minutes, or until

the onions have softened and become golden. Your goal here is to 'melt' the onions not
brown or make them crispy or caramelized. Stir with a wooden spoon, especially at the beginning, beware of the hot bottom of the pot!

Next, sprinkle the flour over them; cook for 4 or 5 minutes, stirring occasionally, then add the red wine. You will want to use your wooden spoon to scrape up all those really good browned bits from the bottom of
the pot.

Once the wine starts to boil, return all the meat and its juices to the pot, along garlic and the cheese cloth bound bundle of fresh herbs. Add stock/water (and two big spoons of demi-glace, if you have it) so the liquid covers the meat by one-third – meaning you want a ratio of 3
parts liquid to 2 parts meat. This is a stew, so you'll need plenty of liquid even after it cooks down and reduces. Bring to a boil, then reduce the heat to medium-low; cook, uncovered, for about 2 hours.

After 2 hours, add the carrots and cook for another 30-60 minutes.

You should pay attention to the dish, meaning to check it every 15 to 20 minutes, stirring and scraping the bottom of the pot to make sure the meat is not sticking or scorching. You should also skim off any foam or scum or oil collecting on the surface, using a large spoon or ladle.
When the boeuf bourguignon is done, discard the cheese cloth bundled herbs, and serve, adding the chopped parsley on top of the bowl of delicious goodness.

Darrel Lewis (Mary Jo's Son)

Venison (Mexican) Meatloaf

2 tablespoons olive oil
1 cup onions, finely diced
2 jalapeno peppers, seeded and minced
6 garlic cloves, minced
1 ½ cups crushed tortilla chips
2 eggs, lightly beaten
1 cup tomato salsa (your choice of mild, medium or spicy)
1 ½ cups fresh corn kernels
1 cup shredded Mexican cheese blend
1 teaspoon chili powder
½ teaspoon dried oregano
¼ teaspoon cumin powder
1 teaspoon salt
1 ½ pounds ground venison, elk, etc.
1 pound lean ground bison
½ pound chorizo sausage, casing removed, crumbled
1 cup sour cream
3 tablespoons ketchup
1 tablespoon lime juice

Directions:
Heat oil in a skillet over medium heat and add onion, jalapeno pepper and garlic. Sauté until onions are translucent. Allow to cool.
In a large bowl, combine tortilla chips with next 8 ingredients and mix well. Add venison, beef, chorizo and cooled onion mixture. Mix all ingredients thoroughly with your hands.
In a lightly oiled loaf pan or baking dish, form into a loaf about 4 inched tall. Bake in a preheated 375 degree oven for 50 minutes or until internal temperature is 155 degrees.
Lightly cover with foil and allow to rest for 10 minutes before serving.

For a sauce, whisk together sour cream, ketchup and lime juice. To serve, either serve on grilled sourdough bread as pictured OR slice meatloaf and arrange on plates.
Note: Try this recipe with ground waterfowl breasts!

Mary Jo Stumreiter (Lewis) Nickum

Joe and Ludwig Stumreiter

Harvest Casserole with Wild Rice

2 pounds Jimmy Dean sausage
1 bunch green onion chopped into the green
1 cup chopped celery
1 cup chopped mixed green, red, yellow, and orange peppers
1 cup sweet potato chopped dime size and partially cooked
1 cup cooked wild rice
1 cup cooked white long grain rice (optional)
1 can Cream of Mushroom soup
1 can Cream of Celery Soup
½ cup milk
½ cup fresh mushrooms or small can (optional)
1 can water chestnuts chopped (optional)

Brown sausage.
Add onion, peppers and celery. Sauté.
Mix remaining items into a large bowl.
Combine all into a large casserole.
Bake at 350 degrees F. for 1.5 hrs. This is even better if left to "mingle" or set in refrigerator one day or more before baking.
Serve with breadsticks, squash and green beans.

This is Chip's (son of Irene Stumreiter Griffin Hinke) favorite Fall meal.

Sweet-Sour Pork

1 ½ pounds lean pork, cut in strips
2 Tbsp. hot oil
1 cup water
1 chicken bouillon cube
1 (20 ounce) can pineapple chunks
¼ cup brown sugar
2 Tbsp. cornstarch
¼ cup vinegar
1 Tbsp. soy sauce
Salt as desired
1 medium green pepper, in 1 inch chunks
¼ cup thinly sliced onion
Cooked rice, as desired

Brown the pork slowly in the hot oil. Add 1 cup water and bouillon cube. Cover and simmer until tender, about 1 hour. Meanwhile, drain the pineapple, reserving syrup. Combine brown sugar and cornstarch, pineapple syrup, vinegar, soy sauce and salt. Cook and stir over medium-high heat until thick and bubbly. Remove from heat. Add sauce over pork; mix well. Stir in pineapple, green pepper and onion. Cook over low heat, 2 to 3 minutes or until vegetables are tender-crisp. Makes 6 servings.

R. E. Westphal

Grandma Amelia and Family

Tortellini for Dating (otherwise known as "the man getting meal")

2 Tbsp. margarine
1 cup mushrooms, chopped
½ cup chopped onion
1 garlic clove, minced
9 oz. cheese tortellini
4 cups spinach, chopped
8 oz. cream cheese, softened
1 tomato chopped to cubes
¼ cup milk
¼ cup parmesan cheese
1 tsp. Italian seasoning
¼ tsp. each salt and pepper
1 lb. Italian sausage
Red wine to your taste

Brown Italian sausage, then drain and set aside.
Sauté mushrooms, onion, and garlic in butter.
Add the rest of the ingredients.
Cook on low until warmed through, about 30 minutes.
Add additional wine or milk as needed for consistency.
Serve with breadsticks and a nice salad, plus wine.
Guaranteed to satisfy your man!

Elizabeth Hinke Sherry (Granddaughter of Irene Stumreiter Griffin Hinke)

Mediterranean Seafood Stew

¼ cup chopped green pepper
2 Tbs. finely chopped onion
1 clove garlic, minced
1 Tbs. cooking oil
1 16-oz. can diced tomatoes
1 8-oz. can tomato sauce
½ cup dry red wine
3 Tbs. snipped parsley
Dash of each salt and pepper
¼ tsp. dried oregano
¼ tsp. dried basil
1 pound fresh or perch fillets (or thawed frozen fillets)
1 7 1/2 oz. can minced clams
1 4 1/2 oz. can shrimp, drained

In large saucepan cook chopped green pepper, onion, and garlic in cooking oil until vegetables are tender but not brown. Add undrained tomatoes, tomato sauce, wine, parsley, salt and pepper, oregano, and basil to saucepan. Bring mixture to boiling. Reduce heat: cover and simmer 20 minutes. Remove skin from perch fillets. Cut fillets into pieces, removing any bones. Add fish to mixture in saucepan; simmer 5 minutes. Add undrained clams and shrimp; continue simmering, covered, about 3 minutes more or until perch is tender. Makes 6 servings in soup bowls.

Bill Westphal

Stir Fried Shrimp with Vegetables

2 medium carrots
1 cup fresh mushrooms
1 pound fresh or frozen shrimp
½ cup chicken broth
1 tablespoon cornstarch
¼ cup low-sodium soy sauce
2 tablespoons cooking oil
1 clove garlic, minced
1 teaspoon ginger
1 cup thinly sliced cauliflower
2 cups chopped bok choy
1 cup fresh pea pods
1 small can water chestnuts

Halve shrimp lengthwise. Blend chicken broth into cornstarch; stir in soy sauce and ginger and set aside. Preheat wok or large skillet over high heat; add oil. Stir fry garlic for 30 seconds. Add cauliflower and carrots for 3 minutes. Add bok choy, pea pods, mushrooms and water chestnuts; stir fry 2 minutes or more until vegetables are crisp-tender.
Remove vegetables to bowl. Add more oil and stir fry shrimp 7 to 8 minutes. Push shrimp away from the center. Stir chicken broth mixture and add to center of skillet. Cook and stir until thick and bubbly. Stir in vegetables; cover and cook 1 minute. Serve at once over rice. Serves 4.

Bill Westphal

Best-Ever Crab Cakes

12 ounces fresh jumbo lump crabmeat, drained and picked over
12 ounces fresh lump crabmeat, drained and picked over
4 ½ tablespoons salted butter, melted and cooled
4 ½ tablespoons chopped scallions (from 4 scallions)
1 ½ tablespoons finely chopped fresh flat-leaf parsley
1 ½ tablespoons finely chopped fresh dill
1 ½ teaspoons lemon zest plus 1 1/2 Tbsp. fresh juice (from 1 lemon)
1 ½ teaspoons kosher salt
1 ½ teaspoons hot sauce (such as Tabasco)
3 large eggs, lightly beaten
1 large garlic clove, minced (about 2 tsp.)
2 ¼ cups panko (Japanese-style breadcrumbs), divided
4 tablespoons canola oil

Prepare the Crab Cakes: Place first 11 ingredients and 1 3/4 cups of the panko in a large bowl, and gently combine. Shape crabmeat mixture into 6 (3-inch) cakes, about 6 1/2 ounces each. Sprinkle remaining 1/2 cup panko on a large plate; gently transfer cakes to plate, pressing both sides in panko. Cover and chill until slightly firm, about 15 minutes. Preheat oven to 375°F. Heat 2 tablespoons canola oil in a large nonstick skillet over medium-high. Gently reshape 3 Crab Cakes, and place in hot oil. Cook until golden brown, 4 to 5 minutes on each side. Transfer to a wire rack set in a baking sheet. Repeat with remaining oil and cakes. Place baking sheet in preheated oven, and bake cakes until heated through, about 10 minutes.

Mary Jo Stumreiter (Lewis) Nickum

Southwestern Turkey Burgers

1 ¼ lbs. Ground turkey
1 tsp. Chipotle chile canned in adobo, chopped
6 T. Fresh cilantro, chopped
1 T. Diced green chiles
¾ C. Chopped green onions
3 tsp. Ground cumin
4 Med. Whole wheat hamburger bun, or ww tortillas
Salsa
Avocado (optional)

Directions:
1. In a medium size bowl, mix turkey, chipotle chile, cilantro, green chiles, green onions, and cumin. Form into four patties.
2. Bring grill to medium high heat. Grill burgers until cooked through, about 4 or 5 minutes each side. Serve burgers atop a whole wheat bun or for a different flair, in four whole wheat tortillas. Add a tablespoon of salsa and a sliver of avocado if desired.

Mary Jo Stumreiter (Lewis) Nickum

Mother and Dad's Wedding

Zucchini Hot Dish

3 cups cubed zucchini
1-1/2 oz. cheddar cheese
4 oz. cooked, diced chicken
1 oz. chopped green onion
3 teaspoons parsley flakes
¼ teaspoon garlic powder
1/8 teaspoon oregano
1 cup tomato sauce
½ oz. Parmesan cheese

Mix all ingredients and place in medium baking dish. Bake at 350 degrees F. for 30 to 35 minutes.

Kareen Mabie England

Zucchini Hot Dish

Sweet Potato and Carrot Soup

4 tbsp. butter
1 large onion, finely chopped
2 large sweet potatoes, peeled and diced
5 large carrots, peeled and diced
1 tbsp. chopped fresh parsley
Juice of one lemon
3-3/4 cups vegetable stock
2 tsp. salt
1 tsp. black pepper
Sour cream (optional)

In a large saucepan, melt the butter and add the onion. Stir until it is transparent. Add the sweet potatoes and carrots. Reduce the heat to very low and cook for 10 to 15 minutes, stirring constantly, until the vegetables are tender. Add the parsley, lemon juice, stock, and salt and pepper. Cover and simmer for 35-40 minutes. Allow to cool slightly, then pour into a blender or food processor and blend until the soup is fairly smooth but retains some texture. Return the soup to the pan and reheat it over very low heat until it's piping hot. Pour into bowls. Top each serving with a dollop of sour cream, if desired. Serve immediately. Makes 6 servings.

R. E. Westphal

Chili

1 pound Hamburger (browned and drained)
2 10oz. can tomato paste
2 15oz. can tomato sauce
1 11oz. can tomato soup
1 15oz. can dark kidney beans drained and rinsed
2 15oz. can light kidney beans drained and rinsed
2 15oz. can chili beans (not drained)
1 tsp. chili powder
¼ tsp. Tabasco sauce
1 Tbsp. Worchester sauce
½ tsp. each salt and pepper
1 Tbsp. brown sugar
¼ tsp. crushed red pepper leaves

Mix together and bring to heat level where it bubbles up. Turn down to a simmer.

Jonathan and Brandon Hinke (Grandsons of Irene Stumreiter Griffin Hinke)

Kitchen Kitty Wisdom

Use uncooked spaghetti for a cake tester.

Zesty Minestrone Soup

1 lb. Hot Italian Sausage- rolled into small balls.
1 bunch green onion chopped
1 cup chopped celery
1 cup chopped green, red, yellow, and orange peppers.
1cup carrots chopped dime size and partially cooked
1 15 oz. can Extra Thick and Zesty tomato sauce
1 15oz. can beef broth
1 - 2cups water depends on what you want for consistency
1 16 oz. bag frozen mixed vegetables (or any other vegetables you want)

Roll sausage into small balls and brown sausage. (drain if necessary)
Add onion, peppers, carrots, veggies and celery.
Pour in sauce and broth, add water.
Heat to boil, then simmer.

Irene Stumreiter Griffin Hinke "one of my favorite Fall soups."

Mary and John Griffin's Wedding

Vegetarian Chili

2 15 oz. cans of Mexican seasoned Pinto beans
2 15 oz. cans Mexican seasoned Tomatoes
1 10 oz. can tomato sauce
1 large onion, chopped
2 Tbsp. Tomato paste
1 cup frozen corn
1 tsp. chili powder
Jalapeños to taste

Combine all ingredients in a slow cooker and cook on high for about 30 minutes then low for 3-4 hours, until flavors are well blended.
Serve with sour cream and corn chips

Mary Jo Stumreiter (Lewis) Nickum

Grandma Amelia and Grandpa Alois

Tortilla Soup

3 cloves garlic
1/2 onion
3 ripe tomatoes
6 cups chicken stock
1-2 tablespoon oil
corn tortillas
2 avocados
1 cup shredded cheddar cheese
Sour cream
Salt and Pepper
1 tsp. Cumin
1 tbs. taco seasoning or Mexican seasoning
1/2 tsp. hot chili powder
Optional: 2 cups shredded chicken

Roast onion, garlic and tomatoes under broiler until brown and bubbling. Put into blender and blend until smooth. Heat oil in a heavy based stock pot, add tomato mixture and sauté until mixture thickens and turns orange in color. Add chicken stock and seasonings and let simmer for at least one hour or at this time it may be placed in a crock-pot on low to cook all day.
Place cheese in a soup bowl add soup, sliced avocados, spoon full of sour cream and top off with purchased tortilla strips.

Mary Jo Stumreiter (Lewis) Nickum

Five-Alarm Chili

NOTE: Put the fire department on standby to put out the "heartburn" when serving this chili. Beware—it's hot!

4 dried ancho chilies stems and seeds removed and flesh torn into 1-inch pieces
3 ½ cups water
1 (28 oz.) can whole peeled tomatoes
¾ cup crushed corn tortilla chips
¼ cup canned chipotle chilies in adobo sauce plus 2 tsps. adobo sauce
2 Tbsps. vegetable oil
2 lbs. lean ground beef
Salt and pepper
2 medium-sized onions, chopped fine
1 jalapeno chili, seeds reserved and minced
4 clove garlic
2 Tbsps. ground cumin
2 Tbsps. chili powder
1 Tbsp. dried oregano
2 tsps. Ground coriander
2 tsps. sugar
½ tsp. cayenne pepper
1-1/2 cups beer
3 (15 oz.) cans pinto beans, rinsed

1. Combine ancho chilies and 1 ½ cups water in a medium microwave-safe bowl and microwave until softened, about 2 ½ to 3 minutes. Drain and discard liquid.
2. Place ancho chilies, tomatoes and their juice, remaining 2 cups of water, tortilla chips, and chipotle in adobo sauce in a blender and process until smooth, about 1 minute. Set aside.

3. Heat 2 tsps. oil in a Dutch oven until oil starts to smoke. Add ground beef, 1 tsp. salt and pepper and cook until well-browned, breaking into pieces with spoon, 10-15 minutes. Drain meat in a colander and set aside.
4. Heat remaining 4 tsps. oil in Dutch oven and add onions and jalapeno with seeds. Cook for approximately 5 minutes, until onion is nicely browned. Stir in garlic, cumin, chili powder, oregano, coriander, sugar, and cayenne and cook until fragrant, about 30 seconds.
5. Pour in beer and bring to a simmer. Add in beans, ancho-tomato mixture, and beef and return to a simmer. Cover and reduce heat to low. Cook 50 to 60 minutes, stirring occasionally.
6. Serve with side of corn bread.

Bill Westphal

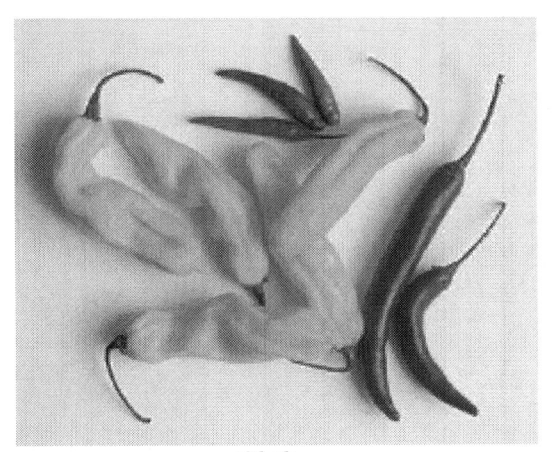

Chilies

Side Dishes

Cucumbers with Sour Cream

1 cup sour cream
1 scant tablespoon sugar
2 tablespoons cider vinegar
¼ cup chopped fresh dill
¼ teaspoon white pepper
½ teaspoon salt
1 teaspoon celery seed
2 long, slender cucumbers
1 small onion
Chopped fresh dill

In a medium bowl, combine the sour cream, sugar, vinegar, dill, pepper, salt, and celery seed; blend. Pare the cucumber and slice as thin as possible. Clean the onion and slice it a bit thicker than the cucumber. Add the vegetables to the sour cream mixture and toss lightly. Refrigerate for at least 2 hours so the cucumbers can absorb the dressing. Sprinkle with additional dill and serve.

Bill Westphal

Cucumbers

Aunt Catherine's Lime Gelatin Salad

1 package lime gelatin dissolved in ¾ cup boiling water; Cool
1 cup whipped cream
1 cup drained canned fruit cocktail or other canned fruit cut in small pieces
1 cup cottage cheese
½ cup chopped nuts if desired

Mix all ingredients together. Just before gelatin sets pour into mold if desired. Better if left overnight.

R. E. Westphal

Grandma's "Reiberdatschi"

8 big potatoes
2 eggs
salt
3 tablespoons Gurnard for baking

Rub the peeled, raw potatoes, drain well or squeeze lightly, stir in the eggs and flour, salt. Put a tablespoon of small "Reiberdatschi" in a pan with hot fat, bake light brown and crispy on both sides. To eat is best with apple compote or sauerkraut.

Katrin Mühlbauer (born Stumreiter)

Rainbow Jello Salad

2-3oz. packages lime jello
5 cups hot water
4 cups cold water
1 package lemon jello
½ cup mini marshmallows
1-1lb. 4oz. can crushed pineapple, drained
1 cup pineapple juice
1-8oz. package cream cheese
1 cup heavy cream, whipped
1 cup mayo
2-3oz. package cherry jello

Dissolve lime jello in 2 cups hot water. Add 2 cups cold water. Pour into a 14x10x2 inch pan or large mold, and chill until partially set.

Dissolve lemon jello in 1 cup hot water in top of double boiler. Add marshmallows and stir until melted. Remove from heat and add 1 cup of drained pineapple juice and cream cheese. Beat until well blended and stir in pineapple. Cool slightly. Fold in whipped cream and mayo. Chill until thickened, then pour in layer over lime jello until set.

Mix cherry jello in 2 cups hot and 2 cups cold water. Chill until syrupy. Pour over other layers. Chill until firm.

Mary Jo Stumreiter (Lewis) Nickum

Marinated Vegetable Salad

1 small head cauliflower
1/3 pound small whole green beans,
<u>Or</u>, 1- 9-ounce package frozen green beans
3 carrots
2 small zucchini
1 cup chopped fresh parsley

<u>Vinaigrette Dressing</u>
½ cup vegetable oil
¼ cup cider or red wine vinegar
3 tablespoons lemon juice
1 teaspoon Worcestershire sauce
1 teaspoon salt
½ teaspoon powered mustard
½ teaspoon coarsely ground black pepper

Wash and break cauliflower into small bite-sized flowerets. Wash and snip green beans or thaw and drain frozen ones. Peel and thinly slice carrots. Wash and thinly slice zucchini. The zucchini, parsley, and frozen green beans do not have to be cooked; blanch the following vegetables separately: cauliflower—6 minutes; fresh green bean—4 minutes; carrots—3 minutes. Transfer the vegetables immediately to ice water to stop cooking. Drain well in a colander and set aside.
Prepare the vinaigrette. In a 2-cup jar, combine the ingredients for the dressing and shake to blend. In a deep 3-quart glass bowl, layer the vegetables in the following order: one-third of the cauliflower, beans, carrots, zucchini, and fresh parsley. Add vinaigrette as you layer and repeat 2 more times. Do not mix together. Cover tightly and refrigerate overnight. Occasionally pour the dressing off into a bowl, then pour it back over the vegetables.
Serves 10-12. This salad can be served from the bowl or on salad plates with lettuce leaves.

R. E. Westphal

Favorite Coleslaw

3 lbs. cabbage shredded (1 regular size cabbage)
1 small green pepper, chopped
1 carrot, shredded
1 cup shredded red cabbage

Dressing:
1 cup sugar
1 tsp. dry mustard
½ cup vegetable oil
2 Tbsp. fresh chopped or dried onion
1 cup cider vinegar
½ tsp. celery seed

Mix all solid ingredients together in a large bowl.
In a saucepan, put all the DRESSING ingredients together. Bring to a rolling boil to dissolve the ingredients. Remove the liquid ingredients from the heat and let cool completely in the pan.

Pour over the top of the solid ingredients, toss liquid with the solid ingredients in the bowl.
Put the coleslaw in the refrigerator for 2 hours.
Re-toss just before serving.

R. E. Westphal

Kaiserschmarrn

1 c. flour
1 pinch salt
1½ c. milk
4 eggs, separated
3 Tbsp. sugar
2 Tbsp. butter
½ c. sultanas (raisins)

Mix flour, salt, milk, egg yolks and sugar.
Beat the egg whites until stiff and folds them gently into the dough.
Add fat to the pan and pour in a portion of the dough.
Sprinkle raisins, fry slowly.
Turn and finish cooking. Continue process with remaining dough.

Liz Kaupp

Wolfgang Stumreiter Family

Irish White Potatoes: Something out of Nothing

When I was young, my tastes outstripped my wallet. I wanted good food, but didn't know how to cook. In desperation I started experimenting with whatever
I could find in the fridge and cupboard. Most of those experiments are best left unremembered, but this one was so good I still cook it 30 years later.

I remember asking my mom what spice goes good with potatoes, and she suggested cumin, and the dish was born! While I won't swear by its nutrition or healthiness, I will swear by the flavor.

Ingredients:
1 15oz can of sliced Irish White Potatoes (drained of water)
1/2 tsp ground cumin
Salt (to taste)
2 Tbs finely chopped Italian (flat) parsley
2 slices of Monterey jack (or other soft white cheese like provolone)
1 Tbsp. Olive Oil

Equipment:
Skillet/Fry Pan w Lid (if no Lid then foil)
wooden spoon

Instructions:
Warm a skillet over medium heat (no hotter!) with the olive oil.

Once hot, empty (remember to drain the water first) can into the skillet.

Add salt and cumin and gently stir to coat the potatoes with the oil and cumin. They should not brown or stick, since we aren't trying to fry the potatoes! After 3-5 minutes the potatoes will be warmed through and the cumin and oil just starting to brown on the outside.

Remove from heat, add slices of cheese to the top of the potatoes, and cover with lid.

After cheese is melted, sprinkle with Parsley and serve! I like to serve this dish as a side along with grilled chicken or grilled salmon, and sautéed spinach.

Darrel Lewis (Mary Jo's son)

Potatoes

Apple-Cabbage Slaw

1 cup plain yogurt
½ cup sour cream
2 Tbsp. honey
½ cup chopped fresh parsley
2 cups shredded napa cabbage
2 cups shredded red cabbage
(1 large bag of shredded slaw can be used instead of both cabbages listed above)
2 cups shredded carrots
½ cup dried cranberries
2 medium apples, cored and finely chopped
3 Tbsp. dried minced onion
Salt and pepper to taste

In a large bowl, whisk together the yogurt, sour cream, honey and chopped parsley. Add all the other ingredients and mix well. Cover and chill until you are ready to enjoy.

R. E. Westphal

Amelia, Alois and family

Tomato Salad - Greek Village Style

I absolutely love making this every summer when tomatoes are at their peak. Most people, and even most restaurants that serve this dish don't highlight the real star of it, the glorious tomato! Don't bother making
this dish if its winter time, use fresh delicious summer tomatoes or don't bother! I disklike green peppers, though those are a traditional ingredient.

This type of cooking, which I love, is found all over the world and I call it (admiringly) 'peasant fair'. The key is fresh ingredients, because there is nothing to hide behind flavor wise. What works is the mix of salt from the olives and cheese mixes with the bright flavors of the vegetables, all coated in a deliciously rich herb dressing. The acid from the lemon is a must.

Ingredients:
 Salad:
4 tomatoes, cut in bite sized wedges
1 slender green cucumber, pealed and cut into chunks
1 green pepper (if you insist) sliced
2 red peppers sliced
1 red onion, sliced
1/2 cup kalamata olives (un-pitted they taste better)
8 ounces feta cheese, sliced

Dressing:
1/4 cup olive oil
1/8 cup of red wine vinegar
2 Tbs fresh lemon juice
1 Tbs fresh oregano
1 teaspoon parsley, chopped
3 garlic cloves, finally minced or crushed
1/2 teaspoon salt

fresh ground black pepper
Equipment:
Large Mixing Bowl
Spoon
Small Mixing Bowl (for dressing)
Chopping Board with sharp Chef Knife

Mix salad ingredients with the exception of the feta. Mix salad
dressing then toss with vegetables, let stand for a 1/2 an hour then add
feta cheese and serve.

I normally don't even really measure when I make this dish. Feel free to
experiment with the quantities of the ingredients above, remembering
that the tomatoes should remain the star of the show!

Darrel Lewis (Mary Jo's sons)
Ryan Lewis

Tomato

Lillian's Three Bean Salad

1 can French cut green beans
1 can yellow wax beans
1 can red kidney beans
1/2 cup minced green peppers
1/2 cup chopped onion
1/2 cup salad oil
1/2 cup vinegar
3/4 cup sugar
1/2 tsp. pepper

A day in advance drain beans and put in bowl with green pepper and onions. Pour the other four ingredients onto mixture. Toss well, cover and refrigerate. Toss again right before serving.

Nancy Stumreiter Zappen

Three Bean Salad

Boletus Mushrooms in Cream Sauce with Pretzel Dumplings

1 lb. boletus mushrooms
1 lb. pretzels, bread type, not crunchy
2 cups milk, warm
6 eggs
1 small onion
1-1/5 cups cooking cream
Garlic, salt, pepper, nutmeg, to taste
Herbs, such as basil, parsley
Olive oil

Sauce:
Cut onion in small pieces and sauté in olive oil. Cut mushrooms into slices and add them to the pan. Stir-fry. Add cooking cream and season with salt, pepper, herbs and garlic. Let everything simmer for a short while.
Dumplings:

Cut pretzels in small pieces. Put them in a bowl and add the warm milk. Add the eggs and season with salt, pepper and nutmeg. Blend well. Shape the mass into a roll and put it into a linen sheet. Tie up the ends and put it into boiling water for approx. 35 min. Subsequently, cut in thick slices and serve with cream sauce.
Enjoy your meal!

Xaver Stumreiter Family

Upper Palatinate Bread Dumplings with Mushroom Cream Sauce

Sauce:
1.3 lbs. mushrooms (preferably porcini, chanterelles and button mushrooms)
1 medium-sized onion
4 tbs. butter
2 tbs. flour
½ bunch parsley
2 cups vegetable stock
1 cup cooking cream
1 cup white wine
White pepper
Salt

Dumplings:
3 rolls from day before (e. g. Kaiser rolls or baguette rolls)
½ medium-sized onion
1 tbs. butter
½ cup hot milk
1 tbs. fresh, small chopped parsley
1 egg
Salt
Pepper
Nutmeg

Sauce:
Clean mushrooms, if possible without water. Cut them in bite-sized pieces. Small mushrooms do not have to be cut. Cut onion into small dices. Heat 2 tbs. butter in a large pan. When melted, add onion dices to the pan and braise lightly. Add mushrooms and parsley. Season with salt and pepper. Stir well. Cook at medium heat with closed lid for 10 min. Melt remaining butter in a second large pan. Stir flour into melted butter and fry until golden brown. Keep stiring and add white wine slowly. Pour vegetable stock into pan and let sauce

simmer for 3 min. Add cooking cream. Subsequently, add mushrooms and stir well. Remove pan from the cooker and season again with salt and pepper, if needed.

Dumplings:
Cut rolls into large cubes. Put them into a large bowl and dash with hot milk. Cover bowl with a plate. Cut ½ onion in small cubes. Put butter into a pan. When melted, add onion dices and braise lightly. Add parsley and braise shortly. Remove pan from cooker. Take plate from bowl and check if bread cubes are softened and milk is absorbed. If not, tear hard bread into small pieces. Squeeze bread so that excess liquid can run off. Put bread into another bowl. Add onion and parsley from the pan. Break the egg into the pan. Season with salt, pepper and nutmeg. Moisten hands with little water and knead until mass is homogenous. Now form dumplings in the size of a soup ladle. Boil water in a cooking pot and add dumplings carefully. Cook for 20 min. Serve with mushroom sauce. For 4 persons.

E. Bittner (neé Stummreiter)

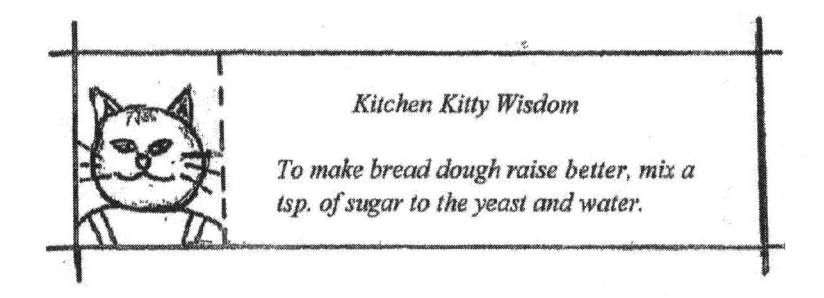

Kitchen Kitty Wisdom

To make bread dough raise better, mix a tsp. of sugar to the yeast and water.

Brown Rice: Easy and Consistently Perfect

Not only is Brown Rice generally considered healthier than white rice, it also just (to me) tastes better. With nutty flavors and a ton of fiber, it holds up well as left overs. Used as a bases for stir-fries, kababs, and perhaps the best of all Brown Rice Pancakes (see below).

Remember that I'm lazy. I wouldn't put anything you don't need in the instructions.

Rice stored in fridge lasts about a week, so this is a staple for a weekend meal that saves time during the work week. Recipe can be adjusted easily if you want more or less rice. My two cups of rice on the weekend lasts my wife and I for about a week.

Ingredients:
2 cup short, medium, or long-grain brown rice
Kosher salt, to taste

Equipement:
Large Stock Pot Strainer

Instructions:
Put 12-16 (or more) cups of water on high heat, covered (so it comes to a boil 25% faster), so it heats up to a boil.

While water is heating, rinse rice in a strainer under cold running water for 30 seconds. The goal here is to be gentle with the rice (so not to break the kernels) but to rinse as much excess starch off the outside of the rice as possible

Once water is boiling, remove lid, then add the rice, stir it once, and boil, uncovered, for 30 minutes. Its during this time that I usually cook the other things for the rest of the meal.

After 30 minutes, remove from heat. Pour the rice into a strainer over the sink. Let the rice drain for 10 seconds, then return it to the pot (off the heat!). Cover the pot and set it aside to allow the rice to steam for 10 minutes.

Uncover the rice, fluff with a fork, and season with salt.

Darrel Lewis (Mary Jo's sons)
Ryan Lewis

Brown Rice

Taco Salad

1 onion, chopped
4 tomatoes, diced
Head of lettuce
1 cup grated cheese
1 avocado
Olives to taste
1 can kidney beans
1 lb. hamburger
½ package taco seasoning
4 oz. bottle of Salsa
Small bag of tortilla chips

Mix onion tomato, lettuce, cheese, avocado and olives together. Set aside.
Brown hamburger with taco seasoning.
Drain and add kidney beans.
Mix hamburger and salad with Salsa. Sprinkle with tortilla chips.

Mary Jo Stumreiter (Lewis) Nickum

Taco Salad

Bread

Aunt Catherine's Bread Biscuits

Dissolve: 2 packages of yeast in ½ cup warm water

Heat to just below boiling:
1 ½ cups milk
½ cup shortening
½ cup sugar
1 tsp. salt

Beat 2 eggs and then add 7 cups flour

Mix together and knead for 10 minutes. Let rise until double in size. Cut dough into size of biscuit desired, place on pan or in muffin tins. Let rise again and then bake in a 375 degree F. oven for 20 minutes or until hollow sounding when tapped.

NOTE: The seven cups of flour may be divided into 2 cups whole wheat and 5 cups white flour.

R. E. Westphal

Mona and Catherine Stumreiter

Cajun Hot Tomato Bread

1 cup Bloody Mary mix
1 cup water
1 package active dry yeast
1/3 cup honey
¼ cup vegetable oil
¼ cup chopped green onion tops
¼ cup chopped parsley
1 clove garlic, pressed
1 tsp. salt
5 to 6 cups all-purpose flour

Combine Bloody Mary mix and water in some saucepan. Cook over low heat until mixture reaches 105 degrees F. to 115 degrees F.; pour into large warm bowl. Add yeast: stir until dissolved. Add honey, oil, onion tops, parsley, garlic and salt; mix well. Add 1 cup flour and stir until smooth. Stir in more flour until firm dough is formed. Knead dough on lightly floured surface about 5 minutes or until smooth and elastic. Shape dough into a ball. Place in greased large bowl; turn to grease sides. Cover bowl and set in warm place to rise about 1 hour or until doubled in bulk.
Punch dough down and divide into two equal pieces. Roll each piece on lightly floured surface into rectangle. Roll each piece tightly from short side, jelly-roll style. Pinch seam to seal; place in greased 9x5x3 inch loaf pan. Cover and set in warm place to rise about 1 hour or doubled in bulk.
Bake in preheated 400 degree F. oven about 30 minutes or until loaves sound hollow when tapped and crust is brown. Remove from pans and cool on wire racks. Makes 2 loaves.

R. E. Westphal

Djanet's Glazed Eggnog Monkey Bread

2/3 cup water
2 eggs
¼ cup butter
3 ½ cups bread flour
1/3 cup sugar
1 tsp salt
1 tsp ground nutmeg
1 ½ tsp bread machine yeast
½ cup chopped pecans

Place all ingredients except pecans in bread machine pan in order recommended by the manufacturer. Select dough/manual cycle - do not use delay cycle. Grease 12 cup Bundt pan. Prepare rum glaze. pour half of glaze into pan, sprinkle with 1/4 cup of the pecans.
Remove dough from pan using lightly floured hands. Divide into 30 equal pieces; arrange in layers over glaze in pan. Pour remaining glaze over dough; sprinkle with remaining pecans. Cover and let rise in warm place about 45 minutes or until doubled. (Dough is ready if indentation remains when touched.)
Heat oven to 350°. Bake 30 to 40 minutes or until golden brown. Let stand 5 minutes. Turn upside-down onto serving plate; leave pan over bread 1-2 minutes to allow glaze to coat bread. Serve warm.

Rum Glaze:
½ cup packed brown sugar
½ cup granulated sugar
1 cup heavy whipping cream
1 tsp rum extract
Mix thoroughly.

Djanet Stumreiter

Mama Irene Griffin Stumreiter Hinke's White Bread

1) Scald 1 cup whole milk, and 1 cup water
2) Add 2 TB sugar, 2 tsp salt, 2 TB Crisco
3) Let cool
4) Mix in 1 yeast + ½ sugar to activate (today dissolve 1 packet of yeast in ¼ cup warm liquid w/ 1 tsp sugar to activate)
5) Mix together with large spoon or in mixer on low, adding little by little 5.5 cups of sifted bread flour.
Before last cup is added, cover surface with some remaining flour and knead dough until it snaps. Once all flour is kneaded into dough, cover with cloth and set in warm spot to rise double, then punch down dough and let rise again. Divide into 3 loafs and put into bread pans. Let rise. Put into preheated oven at 350 degrees for 30 mins.

This recipe can be adapted for Mom's Cinnamon Rolls: Roll out dough after second rising. Sprinkle liberally mixture of cinnamon and sugar to taste, add pats of butter every 4" or so. Roll up dough and cut into 2" pieces. Place cut dough in greased cake pan side by side. Let rise and bake at 325 for ½ hr.

Margo Hinke

Desserts

Whiskey Pecan Cake

11 tablespoons butter (1 stick plus 3 tablespoons)
2 ¼ cups sugar
6 eggs, beaten separately
4 cups sifted self-rising flour
2 teaspoons nutmeg
4 cups pecans, broken
4 ½ cups raisins
½ cup whiskey

Cream butter; add sugar and egg yolks. Combine flour and nutmeg in a bowl. In a small bowl, coat nuts and raisins with a little of the flour mixture; set aside. Alternately add flour mixture with whiskey and beaten egg whites to the creamed mixture. Stir in the coated nuts and raisins. Bake in a greased and floured tube pan or Bundt pan for 2 hours at 275°. A wooden pick or cake tester inserted in center should come out clean.

If you don't have self-rising flour, substitute plain flour using:
1 cup Self-Rising Flour Substitute:
    1 cup (4.25 oz, 119 gr) all-purpose flour (plain flour)
    1 ½ tsp (0.3 oz, 7.5 gr) baking powder
    ¼ tsp (0.05 oz, 1 gr) salt

Mary Jo Stumreiter (Lewis) Nickum

Spud and Spice Cake

1 ¾ cups sugar
1 cup cold mashed potatoes
¾ cup shortening
1 teaspoon cinnamon
½ teaspoon salt
½ teaspoon nutmeg
3 unbeaten eggs
1 cup buttermilk or sour milk
1 teaspoon soda
2 cups plus 2 Tablespoons sifted flour
¾ cup chopped nuts

Combine sugar, potatoes, shorting, cinnamon, salt and nutmeg. Cream mixture 4 minutes on mixer. Add eggs and blend well. Combine soda and buttermilk. Add alternately with the flour to creamed mixture. Add nuts. Bake at 350 degrees F. in a 9 x 13 inch baking dish for 50 to 60 minutes or when toothpick inserted in center comes out clean.

Brown Sugar Frosting

Melt ¼ cup butter. Stir in ¾ cup firmly packed brown sugar. Cook over low heat 2 minutes. Add 3 Tablespoons milk. Bring to a full boil. Cool to lukewarm. Add 2 cups confectioner's sugar. Beat until of spreading consistency.

R. E. Westphal

Banana Nut Bread

1 cup sugar
½ cup shortening
2 eggs
1 teaspoon baking soda
2 cups flour
½ cup chopped nuts
Pinch of salt
3 bananas, mashed

Preheat oven to 350 degrees F. Grease a 9 inch by 5 inch loaf pan.
Combine sugar and shortening and mix until thoroughly blended.
Add eggs separately and stir after each addition. Then add mashed bananas.
Add flour and baking soda mixture and stir just until batter is well combined.
Spoon into loaf pan and bake for 40-60 minutes or until done. Makes 1 loaf.

R. E. Westphal

Banana Nut Bread

Danish Pastry Apple Bars

2 ½ cups flour
1 tsp. salt
1 cup shortening
1 cup sugar
1 tsp. cinnamon
1 egg white
8 to 10 med. Apples
1 egg yolk plus milk to 2/3 cup
1 cup crushed corn flakes cereal

Mix shortening into flour and salt. Add milk/egg yolk mixture; blend with a folk. Roll half of dough to fill a 10 ½ x 15 ½ inch cookie sheet. Sprinkle with crushed cereal flakes. Peel and slice thinly the apples. Place over crust and cereal flakes. Sprinkle with sugar and cinnamon. Roll out other ½ of dough and place on top. Pinch edges together. Beat egg white and brush over top crust. Bake at 400 degrees F. for 60 minutes.

Frosting:
1 cup confectioners' sugar
1 Tbsp. water
½ tsp. vanilla

Mix all ingredients together. If too thick, add a slight amount more water.

R. E. Westphal

Mom's Date Filled Sugar Cookies

Date Filling:
1 package chopped dates
½ can evaporated milk
1 Tablespoon sugar

Mix all ingredients together in a sauce pan and heat over medium heat until thick and bubbly, stirring constantly. Remove from heat and let cool.

Cookie Dough:
¾ cup shortening
1 cup granulated sugar
2 eggs
½ teaspoon vanilla extract
½ teaspoon lemon extract
2 ½ cups flour
1 teaspoon baking powder
1 teaspoon salt

Preheat oven to 400 degrees F. Mix thoroughly shortening, granulated sugar, eggs and flavorings. Blend in flour, baking powder and salt. Cover and chill at least 1 hour. Roll dough 1/8 inch thick on lightly floured surface. Cut into circles about the size of a small doughnut. Before baking, put cookies together in pairs with 1 heaping teaspoon of date filling in the center, (sandwich style). Press edges together with tines of fork. Bake about 8 minutes or until slightly brown around the edges. Makes about 2 dozen.

R. E. Westphal

Old-Fashioned Oatmeal Cookies

1 cup raisins
¾ cup shortening
2 eggs
2 ½ cups flour
1 tsp. soda
1 tsp. cinnamon
2 cups rolled oats
1 cup water
1 ½ c. sugar
1 tsp. vanilla
½ tsp. baking powder
1 tsp. salt
½ tsp. cloves
½ cup chopped nuts

Simmer raisins and water in saucepan over low heat until raisins are plump, 20 to 30 minutes. Drain raisin liquid into measuring cup. Add enough water to make ½ cup.

Heat oven to 400 degrees F. Mix shortening, sugar, eggs, and vanilla. Stir in raisin liquid. Mix in dry ingredients and blend. Add rolled oats, raisins, and nuts. Drop rounded teaspoons of dough about 2 inches apart on ungreased baking sheet. Bake for 8 to 10 minutes or until lightly browned.

R. E. Westphal

Rhubarb Cake with Streusel Topping

1 ½ cups sugar
½ cup margarine or butter
1 egg
1 teaspoon vanilla
2 cups flour
½ teaspoon salt
1 teaspoon baking soda dissolved in 1 cup sour cream
2 cups finely chopped rhubarb

Topping:
¾ cup sugar
1 teaspoon cinnamon
½ cup chopped nuts

Preheat oven to 350 degrees F. Grease and dust with flour a 13 inch by 9 inch cake pan.
In a large bowl, cream sugar and margarine or butter. Beat in one egg until batter is light in color. Add vanilla.
In a separate bowl combine the salt and flour.
Add flour and sour cream mixture alternately starting and ending with flour. Stir until batter is smooth. Add the chopped rhubarb and fold in until well distributed throughout the batter.
Pour batter into cake pan.
Mix topping ingredients together and spread over top of batter.
Bake cake in oven for 45 minutes or until toothpick inserted in center comes out clean. Remove from oven and place on rack to cool completely.

R. E. Westphal

Chocolate Chip Date Cake

Combine: 1 cup chopped dated, 1 teaspoon soda, 1 ½ cups boiling water, and allow to cool.
Cream: ½ cup shortening with 1 cup sugar. Add 2 well-beaten eggs. Stir well and add date mixture.
Sift together: 1 ¼ cups plus 3 Tablespoons flour, ¾ teaspoon soda.
Combine with above mixture. Mix well and pour into a 9 inch by 13 inch greased and floured pan.
Top with the following <u>before</u> baking:
1-- 6 ounce package chocolate chips
½ cup sugar
½ cup chopped nuts
Mix and sprinkle over top. Bake at 350 degrees F. for 45 minutes.

R. E. Westphal

Mama's Molasses Cookies

Blend 1 cup sugar and 1 cup shortening (Crisco) in mixer on low
Add 1 egg, 1 cup molasses, and 2 TB white vinegar (add dash of pepper to cut runs)
Mix in 5 C. all-purpose flour with 1&1/2 tsp. baking soda, 1/2 tsp. salt, 2tsp. ginger, 1 tsp. cloves, 1tsp. cinnamon
Chill 3 hrs.
Roll out 1/4", use cookie cutters
Bake 375 degrees F for 5 mins.

Margo Hinke

Sour Cream Pear Coffee Cake

Streusel:
2/3 cup packed light brown sugar
½ cup all-purpose flour
1 teaspoon ground cinnamon
4 tablespoons margarine or butter, softened
2/3 cup chopped walnuts

Cake:
2 ½ cups all-purpose flour
1 ½ teaspoons baking powder
½ teaspoon baking soda
½ teaspoon salt
1 ¼ cups sugar
6 tablespoons margarine or butter, softened
2 large eggs
1 ½ teaspoons vanilla extract
1 1/3 cups sour cream
3 firm but ripe Bosc pears, peeled, cored and cut into 1 inch pieces

Preheat oven to 350 degrees F. Grease 13 inch by 9 inch baking pan. Dust with flour.
Prepare streusel: In medium bowl, with fork, mix brown sugar, flour, and cinnamon until well blended. With fingertips, work in margarine or butter until evenly distributed. Add walnuts and toss to mix; set aside.
In large bowl, with mixer at low speed, beat sugar with margarine or butter until blended, scraping bowl often. Increase speed to high; beat until creamy, about 2 minutes, occasionally scraping bowl. Reduce speed to low; add eggs, 1 at a time, beating well after each addition. Beat in vanilla. With mixer at low speed, alternately add flour mixture and sour cream, beginning and ending with flour mixture until

batter is smooth, occasionally scraping sides of bowl. With spatula or spoon, fold in pears.

Spoon batter into pan; spread evenly. Sprinkle top with streusel mixture. Bake coffee cake 40 to 45 minutes, until toothpick inserted in center comes out clean. Cool cake in pan on wire rack one hour to serve warm, or cool completely in pan to serve later.

Makes 16 servings.

R. E. Westphal

Large Pearl Tapioca Pudding

Soak ¼ cup of pearl Tapioca overnight in ¾ cup cold water.
Mix 2 cups milk and 1/3 cup plus 1 tbsp. sugar and bring to boil.
Drain water off Tapioca and add to the milk.
Cook and stir till Tapioca is clear.
Then combine 2 beaten eggs, 1/3 cup plus 1 tbsp. sugar and 1/3 tsp. vanilla.
Add to above mixture and bring to full boil. Cool slightly and spoon into individual serving dishes.

Kareen Mabie England

Cowboy Cookies

Into a large mixing bowl add:
2 eggs
1 cup white sugar
1 cup brown sugar
1 cup shortening
1 tsp. vanilla
Mix all above ingredients until smooth.

Add:
2 cups flour
½ tsp. baking powder
1 tsp baking soda
½ tsp. salt
Add this to above mixture and stir until smooth.

Add:
2 cups oatmeal
6 ounces chocolate chips

Mix all together. Bake in a 350 degree F. oven for about 12 minutes. Makes 11 dozen small cookies or 5 to 6 dozen large cookies.

Kareen Mabie England

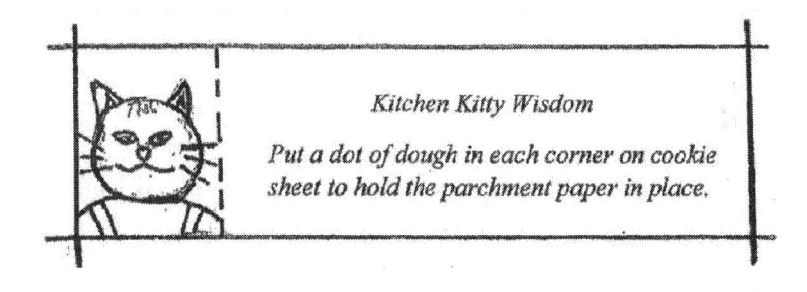

Kitchen Kitty Wisdom

Put a dot of dough in each corner on cookie sheet to hold the parchment paper in place.

Fresh Plum Cake (Zwetschgendatschi)

2 pounds fresh small, blue plums (Italian plums)
1 pkg. dry yeast
1 cup milk, lukewarm
3-1/2 cups flour
1 tsp. Salt
1 cup sugar
¼ cup margarine or butter
1 egg slightly beaten
2 Tbsps. Margarine or butter

Wash and gently cut plums in half and remove the pits.
Sprinkle the yeast into ¼ cup of the milk. Let stand until dissolved.
Mix flour, salt, and 1/3 cup of sugar in a large bowl. Stir dissolved yeast, margarine, egg, and remaining milk into flour.
Knead into a soft dough.
Let rise for 30-40 minutes in a warm place. Punch down and roll on a lightly floured surface into an oblong about 9 inches by 13 inches.
Fit into a greased pan of that size. Pinch edges to make a slight edge around the sides.
Let rise for 20 minutes.
Place plums on top with cut sides up. Sprinkle with remaining sugar; dot with margarine.
Bake in a moderate oven (350 degrees F.) for 35-40 minutes.
Slice and serve warm.

R. E. Westphal

Chip's Zucchini Bread

3 eggs
2 cups sugar
1 cup oil
2 cups grated zucchini
3 tsp. vanilla extract
1 tsp. almond extract
1 tsp. salt
¼ tsp. nutmeg
1 tsp. cinnamon
3 cups flour
1 tsp. baking soda
1 cup chocolate chips
½ cup butterscotch chips
1 cup nuts
½ cup shredded coconut

Mix eggs, oil and sugar.
Add rest of ingredients and blend.
Lastly, fold in nuts and chips.
Bake at 350 degrees F. for about 1 hour. Makes two large loaves.

This is Chip's (son of Irene Stumreiter Griffin Hinke) favorite sweet bread. Irene loves this recipe, also.

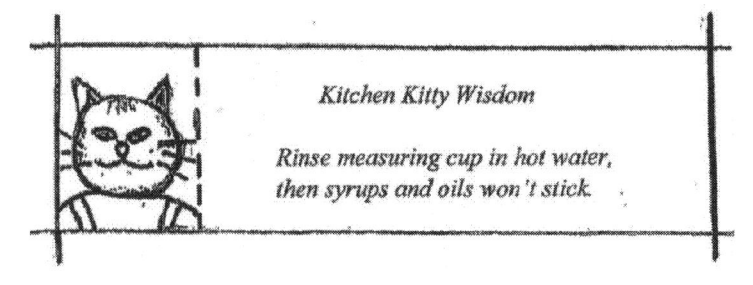

Kitchen Kitty Wisdom

Rinse measuring cup in hot water, then syrups and oils won't stick.

German Buttermilk Sheet Cake

3 cups Sugar
2 cups Buttermilk
4 cups Flour
3 Eggs
1 tsp. Vanilla
1 ½ tsp. Baking Powder

Mix all ingredients until creamy and place in a large baking sheet (13x15 inches) and bake at 320 degrees F. for 20 minutes.
Top with Glaze.

Glaze:
¾ cup Butter
¾ cup Sugar
1 tsp. Vanilla
2-3 tsps. Heavy Cream
1 handful sliced Almonds
1 handful Coconut

Bring Glaze ingredients to a short boil on stovetop and pour on the top of the cake. Bake for additional 10 minutes.

Variation: You can also add fruit i.e. rhubarb, blueberries, red currents to the cake if desired. Place the fruit on top of the batter after it has been poured into the baking sheet prior to baking the first 20 minutes.

Hildegard Stumreiter Kaupp & Annette Kaupp Meffert

Lillian's Favorite Christmas Cookie - Date Ball Cookies

1 cup butter or margarine
1-1/2 cup sugar
2 cups finely chopped dates (1 pound)
2 Tbsp. milk
1 tsp. salt
2 eggs, well beaten
5 or 6 cups Rice Krispies Cereal
1/2 cup chopped walnuts
1 tsp. vanilla
flaked coconut

Melt butter or margarine in a large pan over moderate heat. Add sugar and stir until it is melted. Add dates and continue stirring constantly until the mixture leaves the side of the pan. Stir in milk, salt and eggs. Cook for two minutes. Remove from stove, add cereal, nuts and vanilla. Blend. When the mixture has cooled slightly, rinse hands in cold water and form into balls about the size of a walnut. Roll in coconut and put in refrigerator till set about an hour or two.

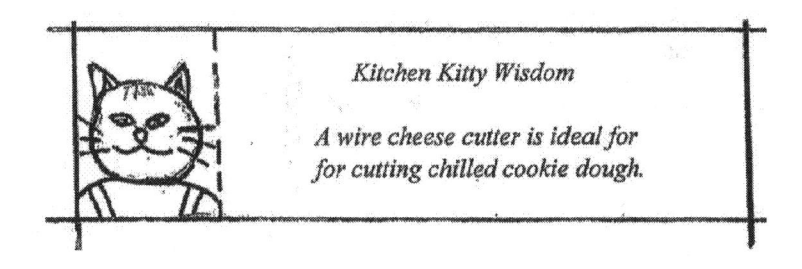

Kitchen Kitty Wisdom

A wire cheese cutter is ideal for for cutting chilled cookie dough.

Lillian's Fruit Bowl Supreme

11 oz. can mandarin orange sections, well drained
8-1/4 oz. can crushed pineapple in syrup, well drained
8 oz. Cool Whip, thawed
2 cups coconut
2 cups mini marshmallows
1/2 cup milk
Combine all ingredients, mixing well. Chill about an hour.

Lillian's Oatmeal Chocolate Chip Cookies

2 cups All Purpose flour, sifted
1 tsp. baking soda
1 tsp. salt
1/2 cup margarine or butter
1/2 cup shortening
1 cup sugar
1 cup firmly packed brown sugar
2 eggs
2 cups quick cooking rolled oats
1 cup chopped almonds or any type nuts
6 oz. semi-sweet chocolate chips

Sift flour with baking soda and salt. Cream butter or margarine in mixing bowl with shortening. Gradually add sugars. Cream until light and fluffy. Blend in eggs. Beat well. Add sifted ingredients, mix thoroughly. Stir in rolled oats, nuts and chocolate chips. Shape dough into balls using a rounded teaspoon for each. Place on ungreased cookie sheets. Bake at 375 for 9-12 minutes until golden. Yield—5 to 6 dozen.

Lillian's Poppy Seed Cake

1 cup butter or margarine, softened
1-1/2 cups sugar
1 can Solo Ground Poppy Seed Filling
4 eggs, separated
1 tsp. vanilla
1 cup dairy sour cream
2-1/2 cups all-purpose flour
1 tsp. baking soda
1 tsp. salt

Preheat oven to 350 degrees F. Grease and flour 12 cup Bundt pan or 10-inch tube pan and set aside.
Beat butter and sugar in large bowl with electric mixer until light and fluffy. Add poppy seed filling and beat until blended. Beat in egg yolks, 1 at a time, beating well after each addition. Add vanilla and sour cream and beat just until blended. Stir flour, baking soda, and salt until mixed, and add to poppy mixture gradually, beating well after each addition.
Beat egg whites in separate bowl with electric mixer until stiff peaks form. Fold beaten egg whites into batter. Spread batter evenly in prepared pan.
Beat 60 to 75 minutes or until cake tester inserted in center comes out clean. Cool in pan on wire rack 10 minutes. Remove from pan and cool completely on rack.
Yield: 14 to 16 serving. Favorite cake for birthdays.

Nancy Stumreiter Zappen

Strawberry Gelatin Pretzel Dessert

Dissolve 1 large box strawberry gelatin in 2 cups hot water. Add 2 cups strawberries, either whole, cut up or mashed. Chill until thick and not set.

CRUST:

1-1/2 cups crushed pretzels using rolling pin
1/2 cup brown sugar
1/2 cup melted butter

Mix and pat into a 9 X 13 baking pan. Bake for 7 min at 325 degrees F.

FILLING:
8 oz. cream cheese
3/4 cup sugar
8 oz. cool whip

Mix cream cheese and sugar together. Add cool whip. Spread mixture over crust and chill.
Lastly, spread gelatin/strawberry mixture which has become thick on the top.

Add more cool whip if desired.

Kareen Mabie England

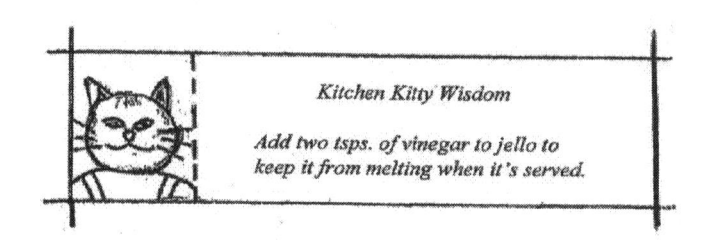

Kitchen Kitty Wisdom

Add two tsps. of vinegar to jello to keep it from melting when it's served.

Miscellaneous

Bill's Plum Liqueur

Wash and dry about 2 ½ quarts of small Italian plums.
Pack into jars.
Put in ¾ cup sugar for each quart; then pour over the plums 1 quart of gin.
Seal jars with lid and ring.
Shake jars once a day until sugar is well dissolved.
Drink is ready 3 months after day it was made. Enjoy!

Note: Other fruits can be used in this recipe---be creative!

Bill Westphal

Best Pie Crust

 5 1/2 cups flour
 1 pound lard
Mix until it looks like pie crust.
NOW:
Add one 12 oz can 7 up or any clear carbonated beverage. Keep mixing. It will look like soup. I use my Kitchen Aid Mixer.
It will soon look like pie crust again. I divide it at least 4 ways, but it depends on how big the pie pans you are using Usually 5 or 6 crusts are made from this dough. I wrap a few crusts for later and freeze.
This is so easy to work with.

Kareen Mabie Englund

Cranberry Celery Seed Salad Dressing

2/3 cup sugar
5 Tbs. honey
1 tsp. salt
1 Tbs. onion
1 Tbs. celery seed
1 tsp. paprika
1 Tbs. lemon juice
1 Tbs. dry mustard
1/3 cup cranberry vinegar*
½ cup water
¾ cup cranberries
¾ cup salad oil

Combine vinegar, water, cranberries and onion in blender and blend on high one minute. Pour into saucepan and mix in all ingredients <u>except</u> oil. Heat and stir over medium heat until sugar dissolves.
Pour into quart jar, add oil and shake well. Can be made ahead and refrigerated. This is wonderful on a spinach salad.

*Cranberry Vinegar

1 cup halved cranberries
2 cups white vinegar

Place in a jar and let sit on the counter for 1 to 2 weeks. Strain through coffee filter or cheese cloth. Use for the salad dressing above.

Bill Westphal

Bavarian Obatzda (cheese spread)

1/2 lb. Brie cheese
2 tbs. butter
2 tbs. onion (finely diced)
2 tbs. sour cream
¼ tsp. ground hot red pepper
1 tsp. ground sweet red pepper
2 pinches black pepper, freshly ground
1 pinch ground caraway
¼ tsp. sea salt
½ tsp. medium-strength mustard
1 oz. pale / lager beer

Decoration: chives and onion rings

Take Brie out of refrigerator and cut off the rind. Cut into pieces. Let ingredients reach room temperature. Mash all ingredients, besides chives, with a fork and blend. Sprinkle with chives and onion rings. Serve cold with Bavarian pretzels or bread.

S. Stummreiter

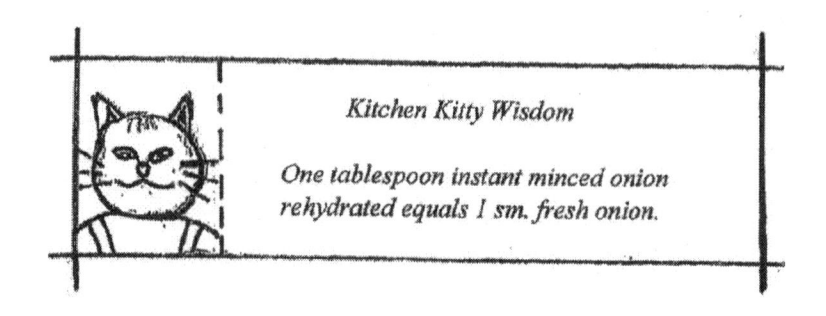

Kitchen Kitty Wisdom

One tablespoon instant minced onion rehydrated equals 1 sm. fresh onion.

Brown Rice Pancakes

These are not only delicious, they are healthy and filling. Feel free to experiment with this one, but keep it health with nuts or a little bit of fruit. Don't sub out the coconut oil, the flavor works perfectly with the nutty brown rice. I've included the brand name of the sugar free syrup that we like (orderable on Amazon), since we really try to minimize our sugar intake.

Ingredients:
Leftover Brown Rice (from the recipe pg. 58)
1-2 eggs per serving (person)
1/8 tsp of cinnamon per serving
1 Tbsp. of coconut oil.
Walden Farms calorie free Pancake Syrup

Equipment:
Small-Medium Mixing Bowl
Skillet/Fry Pan

Instructions:
In a small mixing bowl, beat one egg until yoke and whites are integrated.

Begin adding brown rice in 1/4 cup increments. After each 1/4 cup, stir into rice. As you stir, the starch from the rice will start to thicken the eggs. Keep adding rice, and stirring well, until mix has a consistency of wet porridge.

When enough rice has been added mix in the cinnamon.

Now heat your skillet on medium heat (not hotter!) with the coconut oil.

When hot, ladle out egg mixture into small pancakes, using a spatula to shape, if necessary, into nice round shapes. Cook for a few minutes until golden brown and flip.

When brown on both sides, serve with syrup. You can add chopped nuts to the mix, or make a simple sauce of microwave-thawed frozen blueberries.

Note: 1 egg mixed, usually makes about 3-4 small pancakes, or enough to fit in a large skillet and feed 1 person.

Darrel Lewis (Mary Jo's son)

Brown Rice Pancakes

Microwave Nut Brittle

1 cup granulated sugar
½ cup light corn syrup
1 ½ cups salted peanuts
1 tablespoon butter
1 teaspoon baking soda
1 teaspoon vanilla extract

Instructions

Spray a wooden spoon (or other heat-proof stirring implement) with non-stick cooking spray. Lightly grease a baking sheet, or line it with parchment.
Mix together the sugar and corn syrup in a large microwave-safe bowl and stir until well combined; the mixture will be stiff and hard to stir. Be sure to use a large enough bowl; the sugar/corn syrup should fill it no more than 1/4 to 1/3 full. Microwave the sugar mixture uncovered on high power for 5 minutes; it will bubble vigorously.
Add the peanuts and butter, and stir well to combine. Speed is key! The cooler the mixture becomes the harder it will be to stir.
Replace the bowl in the microwave and cook on high for 2 to 4 minutes, until the mixture turns a nice medium-brown caramel color. Start watching carefully around the 2-minute mark, and remove when the caramel color is achieved.
Add the baking soda and vanilla. The mixture will bubble furiously upon the addition of these ingredients — this is what gives the candy its hallmark airy texture. (This is also why you need to use a large bowl.) Stir quickly to combine. The finished mixture will look creamy and caramelized.
Working quickly, pour the mixture onto your prepared baking sheet and spread it as evenly as possible. If you end up with

an uneven spread, don't worry — the candy should still set up nicely, even in the thicker areas.

When the brittle has set and cooled (30 to 60 minutes), break it into pieces.
Yield: about 3 dozen pieces.

Mary Jo Stumreiter (Lewis) Nickum

Outrageous Granola

3 cups old fashioned oatmeal
1 cup chopped nuts
1 cup dried fruit
2 tsp. vanilla
1-1/2 tsp. cinnamon
1/3 cup brown sugar
1 cup pure maple syrup

Preheat oven to 325degrees F. Mix all ingredients in a large bowl. Transfer to baking sheet sprayed with non-stick butter-flavored spray. Bake for 35-45 minutes, stirring once half way through cooking time. Allow to cool completely on tray. Store in airtight container.

Mary Jo Stumreiter (Lewis) Nickum

Citrus Habanero Glaze

½ c. onion very finely chopped
2 tbsp. olive oil
½ tsp. garlic
¼ tsp. salt
½ tsp. black pepper
½ habanero finely chopped (seeded)
½ c. lime or lemon juice (fresh squeezed preferably)
½ c. orange juice (fresh squeezed preferably)
1 tsp. tamarind paste
3/4 c. apricot preserves
2 tbsp. sugar

Sauté onions, garlic, olive oil and salt for a few minutes. Add the black and habanero pepper sauté for a minute more. Mix in the rest of the ingredients with a whisk and simmer for 15 to 20 minutes, stirring often, until thickened. Make sure it is not too thick because it will thicken in the cooling process. Remove from heat and cool. Use as a glaze on pork or chicken.

Note: If you do not like hot and spicy do not use habanero peppers they are extremely hot. **Substitute quarter of a seeded jalapeno.**

Mary Jo Stumreiter (Lewis) Nickum

Grandma's Potato Pancakes with Apple Compote

Potato pancakes:
2.2 lbs. potatoes, floury
1 onion
3 eggs
1 pinch salt
2 tbs. flour
Canola oil

Apple compote:
1.7 lbs. apples
1 tbs. lemon juice
1 cup water
2 tbs. sugar
½ tsp. cinnamon

Potato pancakes:
Peel potatoes and grate them finely. Put the grating on a kitchen towel and squeeze in order to get the starch out of it. Chop onion in small pieces and add them to the grating. Add eggs, salt and flour and stir well. Heat oil in a pan, form flat pancakes out of the grating and fry them crispy.

Apple compote:
Combine lemon juice and water in a bowl. Wash, peel, quarter and core apples. Cut them into slices and add them to the lemon water. Add sugar and cook at medium heat for 15 – 20 min. Sprinkle with cinnamon. Serve hot or cold. For 3 persons.

S. Stummreiter

Xaver Stumreiter Family

Inhaltsverzeichnis

Hauptspeisen   **98**
    Gefüllte Kalbsbrust   99
    Hühnerfrikaßee   100
    Pichelsteiner   101
    Rahmgulasch   102
    Reißeintopf mit Sellerie   103
    Schweiners mit Kartoffelknödel   104
    Geflügelleber mit Pilzen und Reis   105
    Herzhafte Hackfleischpastete   106
    Huhn gedünstet mit Wein   107
    Kartoffelgulasch   108
    Mama's Hackfleischpfanne   109
    Nudeltopf   110
    Oberpfälzer Schwammerlbrühe mit Semmelknödel   111
    Rinderfilet mit Apfel-Käse-Kruste   113
    Sabrina's Lieblings-Rinderrouladen mit Kartoffelpüree   114
    Steinpilze in Rahm mit Breznknödel   116

Beilagen   **117**
    Lauch – Kartoffel – Auflauf   118
    Marinierter Gemüsesalat   120
    Oma's „Reiberdatschi"   121
    Preiselbeer-Selleriesamen-Salatdreßing   122
    Bayrischer Obatzda   123
    Gurken mit Sauerrahm   124
    Gurkengemüse in Buttersoße   125
    Heißes Tomatenbrot nach Cajun-Art   126
    Oma's Reiberdatschi mit Apfelkompott   128
    Rosenkohltopf   129
    Sellerieschnitzel   130

Tante Catherine's Limonen-Götterspeise-Salat	131
Weißbierkiachal	131

Nachspeisen	**132**
Altmodische Haferflockenkekse	133
Bay Pfannkuchen	134
Bayrisch Creme	135
Gewürzkuchen	136
Grießschnitten	137
Linzer Sternchen	138
Mama's mit Datteln gefüllte Zuckerkekse	139
Riegel aus Apfel-Plundergebäck	140
Schokoladensplitter-Dattel-Kuchen	141
Elisenlebkuchen	142
Kaiserschmarrn	143
Blaubeereis mit Joghurt	143
Bananen-Nuß-Brot	144
Bill's Pflaumenlikör	145
Holländische Mandelkekse	146
Orangenkuchen, Zitronenkuchen	147
Rote Gruetze	148
Scheiterhaufen	149
Schneefloeckchen	150
Schokoladenkuchen (Abruzzen)	151
Zitronen-Gugelhupf	152
Der Kolmsteiner Hof	**155**
The Kolmsteiner Hof	156
Der Kolmsteiner Hof	157
About the Editors	**159**

Hauptspeisen

Gefüllte Kalbsbrust

1,5 kg. Kalbsbrust
1 Zwiebel
50 g. Fett
1 Bund Wurzelwerk
Salz und Pfeffer
Zum Binden:
1/8 l. Weißwein, 6 Eßlöffel Sauerrahm, ca. 30 g. Stärkemehl
Fülle:
3-4 geschnittene alte Semmeln
¼ l. warme Milch
3 Eier
Salz
1 Zwiebel
2 EL Fett
2 EL gehackte Petersilie

Für die Fülle Semmeln mit warmer Milch übergießen und mit Eiern vermengen.
Zwiebeln feinhacken, im Fett andünsten und mit der Petersilie zur Semmelmaße geben.
Alles gut durchmischen.
Tasche in Kalbsbrust schneiden, innen und außen mit Salz und Pfeffer einreiben.
Die Fülle in die Fleischtasche geben und verschließen.
Auf allen Seiten gut anbraten. Zwiebel und Wurzelwerk mitdünsten.
Mit wenig Flüßigkeit aufgießen.
Im vorgeheizten Backofen bei ca. 200 Grad etwa 1 ½ Stunden braten.
Mit Weißwein, Sauerraum und Speisestärke binden und abschmecken.

Maria Haake

Hühnerfrikaßee

1 Suppenhuhn
Suppengrün:Karotten, Lauch, Sellerie, Zwiebel
3 Lorberblaetter
2 l. Salzwaßer
2 st.Zitronenschale
Soße:
40 gr. Butter
40 gr. Mehl
1/2 -3/4 l. Huehnerbruehe
1 Eigelb
1/8 l. Sahne
Zitronensaft
100 gr. Champignons
100 gr. Erbsen
100 gr. Spargel
1 Eßl.Kapern

Huhn in kochendem Salzwaßer mit Lorbeerblatt und Zitronenschale weichkochen,nach ca.1 std.Suppengemuese dazugeben,und nochmal 1 Std.weiterkoecheln, Huhn abtropfen laßen, enthäuteten,entbeinen und in Portionßtuecke teilen.
Für die Soße aus Butter und Mehl helle Einbrenne herstellen, mit Huehnerbruehe aufgießen,10 min.kochen laßen und fleißig umrühren, Eigelb mit Sahne verquirlen und in die Soße rühren,.nicht mehr kochen laßen, Champignons(Dose),gek.Erbsen, Spargel(Dose), Kapern, Huehnerfleisch dazugeben, mit Zitronensaft oder Wein und evtl. Salz abschmecken.

Rita Stumreiter

Pichelsteiner

500 gr. Schweinefleisch(Rindfleisch)
100 gr. Speck
50 gr. Fett
1 Zwiebel,
500 gr. Kartoffeln
1 kg. verschiedene Gemuese:
Petersilienwurzel,Lauch,Karotten
Salz, Paprika, Kuemmel, Petersilie
1/2 l. Gemuesebrurhe

Fleisch und Kartoffeln in grosse Wuerfel, Gemuese in kleine Wuerfel schneiden, Speck mit Zwiebel und Fleisch anbräunen, mit Salz und Paprika würzen,Kartoffeln und Gemuese lagenweise einschlichten, dazwischen immer leicht würzen, als oberste Lage Kartoffeln einschichten, salzen, Kuemmel und Petersilie dazugegeben, seitlich mit Bruehe etwas aufgießen, während der Garzeit hin und wieder aufgießen, nicht umrühren.
Garzeit ca.35 min., bei Rindfleisch ca.45 min.

Rita Stumreiter

Rahmgulasch

500 gr. Kalbfleisch
3 große Zwiebeln
1/2 Teeloeffel Rosenpaprika
1/2 l Waßer
Eßig oder Zitronensaft
250 gr. Sauerrahm
1 Prise Zucker
Salz
1-2 Teeloeffel Delikateßpaprika

Kalbfleisch in gleichgroße Stuecke schneiden, Zwiebel kleinschneiden und in etwas Fett anbräunen, Fleisch dazugeben und mit Rosenpaprika würzen, Waßer dazugeben, das Gulasch wird zugedeckt halbweich geschmort, dann mit etwas Eßig oder Zitronensaft und Sauerrahm aufgegoßen, mit Zucker, Salz und Delikateßpaprika abschmecken.

Rita Stumreiter

Max und Schwester

Reißeintopf mit Sellerie

4 – 5 EL Öl
2 Zwiebeln
1 mittelgroße Sellerieknolle
250 – 375 g. Hackfleisch (gemischt)
Salz, 3 -5 EL Tomatenmark
Etwas ¼ l. Brühe
2 EL Rahm
250 – 300 g. Hartreis
Reichlich Salzwaßer
Zum Anrichten: 30 g geriebenen Käse und gehackte Petersilie

Feingeschnittene Zwiebeln in Öl glasig dünsten
Kleinwürfelig geschnittenen oder geraspelten Sellerie
zugeben, gut ausdünsten
Dann das Hackfleisch beifügen, kurz durchdünsten
Tomatenmark und Salz beigeben und mit wenig Flüssigkeit
aufgießen
Zugedeckt bei mäßiger Hitze 15 – 20 Minuten garen
Bei Bedarf restliche Flüßigkeit zugeben, gut abschmecken
In der Zwischenzeit Reis waschen, brühen, in reichlich
kochendem Salz Waßer sprudelnd kochen
bis er gar aber noch körnig ist, höchstens aber 20 Minuten
Garzeit dann abgießen, überbrausen, gut abtropfen laßen, mit
Fleischsoße mischen
Noch etwa 10 Minuten durchziehen laßen, pikant
abschmecken
Reichlich mit Käse und Petersilie bestreut anrichten.
Beilage: Blattsalate

Maria Haake

Schweiners mit Kartoffelknödel

Schweiners:
Schweinefleisch waschen und in Bratreine legen, mit Salz, Pfeffer und Kümmel würzen.
1 Teelöffel Salz und 1/2 Würfel Bratensaft, geviertelten Zwiebel dazulegen und mit Waßer ca. 1 cm hoch aufgießen.
In den vorgeheizten Backofen bei ca. 150°C – 200 °C schieben. Immer wieder aufgießen.
Nach ca. 1 - 1 1/2 Std. ganz aufgießen und Soße nach Bedarf mit Salz und Maggi abschmecken.

Knödel: für ca. 3 - 4 Personen
7 Semmeln in kleine Stücke schneiden
8-10 große Kartoffel schälen und reiben, Saft von den Kartoffeln abgießen.
Anschließend mit Salz würzen, wenn Teig zu dick, etwas Waßer zugeben.
Dann Kugeln mit 5 -7 cm Durchmesser formen.
Im kochenden Salzwaßer ungefähr 25 Minuten kochen lassen.
Als Beilage ist Sauerkraut oder Kartoffelsalat zu empfehlen.

Kathrin Stumreiter

Geflügelleber mit Pilzen und Reis

250 (300) gr. Hartreis
reichlich Salz Waßer
250 gr. Gefluegelleber
40 gr. Butter oder Oel
1-2 Zwiebeln
150 gr Champignons oder andere Pilze
1 Eßloeffel Mehl
1/8 ltr. Bruehe
Etwas Weißwein
2-4 Eßloeffel Sahne
Salz

Reis waschen, in reichlich Salzwaßer 20 min. kochen, abseihen, sehr gut abtropfen lassen und im vorgeheizten Backofen warm stellen.
Gefluegelleber waschen, in etwas kalte Milch legen, dann in feine Scheiben schneiden. Pilze putzen, waschen, in Scheiben schneiden. Feingeschnittene Zwiebel in Butter oder Oel andünsten, Pilze dazugeben, dünsten bis der Saft eingesogen ist, Leberscheiben zugeben, andünsten, dann mit wenig Mehl Überstauben, kurz anrösten, mit Bruehe ablöschen, ein paarmal gründlich aufkochen lassen, Sahne und Wein dazugeben und mit Salz abschmecken, locker unter den heißen Reis Mengen und sofort servieren.

Rita Stumreiter

Herzhafte Hackfleischpastete

3 Taßen gekochtes, geschnetzeltes Rindfleisch, mit der Küchenmaschine
 zerkleinern
3 Äpfel, in dünne Scheiben schneiden
1 Taße Rosinen
1/2 Taße braunen Zucker
3 Eßlöffel Eßig
Rindfleischsaft, um die Füllung zu wäßern

Mische die oben genannten Zutaten und erhitze sie gut.

Füge zur Mischung folgendes hinzu:
1/2 Teelöffel Salz
1/4 Teelöffel Pfeffer
1/2 Teelöffel Muskatblüte
1/2 Teelöffel Nelkenpfeffer
1 Teelöffel Zimt
1/2 Teelöffel Muskat
1/2 Teelöffel Nelke
Mische alles zusammen und erhitze es. Fülle alles in eine ungebackene
Kuchenkruste, lege die Kuchenabdeckung oben drauf und drücke mit dem
Daumen die Ränder ein, sodass nichts herauslaufen kann. Backe die
Pastete bei 220 °C für 30 - 40 min.
HINWEIS: Für dieses Rezept eignet sich sehr gut Wildfleisch.

R. E. Westphal

Huhn gedünstet mit Wein

1 Masthuhn, Salz, etwas Pfeffer
Kräuter nach Wahl wie etwa Salbei, Rosmarin
wenig Thymian, fein gewiegt

zum Duensten:
40 gr. Butter oder Oel
2 Zwiebeln
100 gr. Champignons
1/8 ltr. Bruehe
1/4 ltr. Weißwein oder Rotwein
1/2 Eßloeffel Mehl

Huhn Vierteln, mit Wuerzmischung aus Salz, Pfeffer, und Kräutern von allen Seiten einreiben, in heißem Fett goldbraun anbräunen, fein geschnittene Zwiebel beifügen, glasig duensten, mit wenig Fleischbruehe aufgießen, zugedeckt bei mäßiger Hitze fast fertig garen lassen, dann blättrig geschnittene Champignons zugeben, durchduensten, nach und nach mit Wein aufgießen und fertig garen;
Garzeit ca. 3/4 - 1 1/4 Std., je nach Groeße des Huhns. Wenn Huhn weich ist, Soße mit Mehlteiglein binden, aufkochen laßen, pikant abschmecken, Huhn in Soße anrichten.

Rita Stumreiter

Kartoffelgulasch

600 gr. Kartoffeln
100 gr. durchwachsener Speck
250 gr. Schinkenwurst
2 Paar Wiener Wuerstchen
1 rote und 1 grüne Paprikaschote
3 Zwiebeln
1 Taße Tomatenketchup
2 Eßloeffel Paprikapulver
Salz
Pfeffer
1 Eßloeffel Majoran
1 Spritzer Worcestersauce
1/2 ltr. Fleischbruehe
1 Bund Schnittlauch

Die Kartoffel schälen und in Wuerfel schneiden, Speck würfeln, Schinkenwurst in Stuecke schneiden, Wiener Wuerstchen in Scheiben schneiden, Paprikaschoten putzen-waschen-in Streifen schneiden, in einem großen Topf den Speck auslaßen und dann die übrigen Zutaten dazugeben und einige Minuten heiß werden laßen, mit Tomatenketchup ablöschen und durchrühren, mit Salz, Pfeffer, Majoran, Paprika und Worcestersauce würzen, mit heißer Fleischbruehe auffüllen und 20 min. zugedeckt köcheln laßen, vor dem Servieren mit frisch geschnittenem Schnittlauch bestreuen.

Franzi Sweekhorst/Stumreiter

Mama's Hackfleischpfanne

40 g. Fett
400 g. Hackfleisch
3 große Zwiebeln
2-3 Paprika
geschälte Tomaten
1 Taße Reis
3 Taßen Waßer
Salz, Paprika, Knoblauchzehe, Kräuter

Zwiebeln fein hacken und in heißen Fett glasig dünsten, dann Fleisch zugeben und unter ständigem Wenden anbraten. Dann das geputzte, geschnittene Gemüse zufügen.
1 Taße Reis zugeben, alles andünsten, mit Waßer aufgießen, würzen und zugedeckt ca. 20 Minuten garen laßen.

Katharina Stumreiter

Nudeltopf

250 gr. gekochten Schinken oder beliebige Wurst oder gekochtes Huhn
2 Zwiebeln
1 rote und 1 grüne Paprikaschote
1 Salatgurke
3 Eßloeffel Butter oder Oel
1 Taße Rotwein
3/4 ltr. Fleischbruehe
Salz, Pfeffer aus der Muehle
1 Prise Zucker
1 Teeloeffel Thymian
1 Meßerspitze Muskat
250 gr. gekochte Eiernudeln
1 Taße saure Sahne
1 Bund Estragon

Schinken in Streifen schneiden, Zwiebeln in Streifen schneiden, Paprika ebenfalls in Streifen schneiden, Salatgurke schälen, halbieren und in Scheiben schneiden.

Fett in einem großen Topf geben und die Zutaten darin glasig schwitzen, mit Rotwein ablöschen und mit Fleischbruehe auffüllen, mit Salz, Pfeffer, Thymian, Muskat und Zucker abschmecken. Bei mittlerer Hitze 25 min zugedeckt köcheln lassen. Die gekochten Eiernudeln in den Eintopf geben und das ganze erhitzen, dann die Sahne unterziehen und mit Estragon bestreuen.

Maria Haake

Oberpfälzer Schwammerlbrühe mit Semmelknödel

Soße:
600 g. Schwammerl (am besten Steinpilze, Pfifferlinge und Champignons)
1 mittelgroße Zwiebel
4 EL Butter
2 EL Mehl
½ Bund frische Petersilie
500 ml. Gemüsebrühe
1 Becher Sahne
0,2 l. Weißwein
Pfeffer (weiß)
Salz

Knödel:

3 ein Tag alte Semmeln
½ mittelgroße Zwiebel
10 g. Butter
100 ml. heiße Milch
1 EL frische, klein gehackte Petersilie
1 Ei
Salz
Pfeffer
Muskat

Soße:
Reinige die Pilze, möglichst ohne Waßer. Schneide sie in mundgerechte Stücke. Kleine Pilze müssen nicht geschnitten werden. Schneide die Zwiebel in kleine Würfel. Erhitze 2 EL Butter in einer Pfanne. Wenn die Butter geschmolzen ist, füge die Zwiebelwürfel hinzu und dünste sie leicht an. Füge die Pilze und die Petersilie hinzu. Würze alles mit Salz und

Pfeffer. Rühre alles gut um. Koche die Soße bei mittlerer Hitze bei geschloßenem Deckel für 10 min. Schmelze die übrige Butter in einer zweiten, großen Pfanne. Rühre das Mehl in die geschmolzene Butter und brate es gold-braun an. Rühre weiter um und füge den Weißwein langsam hinzu. Gieße die Gemüsebrühe in die Pfanne und lasse die Soße für 3 min. köcheln. Füge die Sahn hinzu. Anschließend die Pilze hinzufügen und gut umrühren. Nehme die Pfanne vom Herd und schmecke mit Salz und Pfeffer ab.

Knödel:

Schneide die Semmeln in große Würfel. Lege sie in eine große Schüßel und übergieße sie mit heißer Milch. Decke die Schüßel mit einem Teller ab. Schneide die ½ Zwiebel in kleine Würfel. Gebe die Butter in eine Pfanne. Wenn diese geschmolzen ist, füge die Zwiebelwürfel hinzu und dünste sie leicht an. Füge die Petersilie hinzu und dünste sie kurz mit. Entferne die Pfanne vom Herd. Nehme den Teller von der Schüßel und überprüfe, ob die Brotwürfel aufgeweicht sind und die Milk aufgesogen wurde. Wenn nicht, reiße das harte Brot in kleine Stücke. Drücke das Brot aus, sodaß die überschüßige Flüßigkeit ablaufen kann. Lege das Brot in eine andere Schüssel. Füge die Zwiebeln und die Petersilie von der Pfanne hinzu. Schlage das Ei in die Pfanne. Würze mit Salz, Pfeffe und Muskat. Befeuchte die Hände mit ein wenig Waßer und knete den Teig zu einer homogenen Maße. Forme nun Knödel in der Größe einer Suppenkelle. Bringe Waßer in einem Kochtopf zum Kochen und lege die Knödel vorsichtig hinein. Koche sie für 20 min. Serviere sie mit der Pilzsoße. Für 4 Personen.

E. Bittner (neé Stummreiter)

Rinderfilet mit Apfel-Käse-Kruste

6 Scheiben Rinderfilet
Salz und Pfeffer
Fett zum Braten
1 Apfel
200 g. Emmentaler Käse
100 g. Sauerrahm
1 Eigelb

Filet ein bisschen mit Salz und Pfeffer würzen und im heißen
Fett bis zum gewünschten Garpunkt braten.
Apfel schälen und raspeln, Käse klein reiben.
Apfel und Käse mit Eigelb und Sauerrahm vermischen.
Filet mit der entstandenen Maße bestreichen und bei starker
Hitze im Backrohr braten.

Silvia Stumreiter

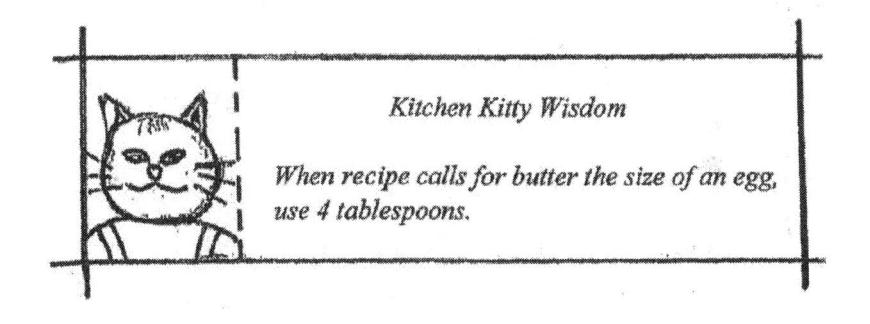

Kitchen Kitty Wisdom

When recipe calls for butter the size of an egg, use 4 tablespoons.

Sabrina's Lieblings-Rinderrouladen mit Kartoffelpüree

6 Rinderrouladen
1 kleines Glas Eßiggurken
1 kleine Packung Speckwürfel
1 Tube mittelscharfen Senf
1 Bund Suppengemüse (Karotte, Sellerie, Poree)
2 mittelgroße Zwiebeln
1 Tube Tomatenmark
250 ml. Kochsahne
Salz
Pfeffer
Olivenöl
Rotwein
Waßer
Butterschmalz

Kartoffelpüree:
1 kg. Kartoffeln
250 ml. Milch
30 g. Butter
Salz
Muskat

Wasche und tupfe das Fleisch ab, würze es mit Salz und Pfeffer und bestreiche es mit dem Senf. Hacke die Eßiggurken und 1 Zwiebel so klein wie möglich und verteile sie auf den Rouladen. Verteile die Speckwürfel ebenfalls auf den Rouladen. Rolle die Rouladen zusammen und fixiere sie mit Zahnstochern.

Brate sie in einer Kaßerolle scharf an und nehme sie dann wieder heraus. Hacke das Suppengemüse in grobe Stücke, brate es gut im Bratfett der Rouladen an und füge ein wenig Tomatenmark hinzu. Lege die Rouladen zurück in die Kaßerolle und gieße sie mit Waßer und Wein auf bis die

Rouladen zu ¾ mit Flüßigkeit bedeckt sind. Stelle die Kaßerolle nun mit Deckel für 2 Stunden in den vorheizten Ofen und schmore die Rouladen bei 180°C. Wenn nötig, Waßer und Wein nachgießen.
Anschließend die Rouladen aus der Kaßerolle nehmen. Füge die Kochsahne zur Flüßigkeit hinzu und püriere alles, um eine exzellente Soße zu erhalten.

Für das Kartoffelpüree: Schäle und wasche die Kartoffeln. Schneide sie in große Stücke. Koche sie in Salz Waßer für 20 – 25 min. Gieße das Waßer ab. Stelle den Kochtopf zurück auf die warme Herdplatte, bedecke ihn und laß das übrige Waßer verdampfen bis die Kartoffeln trocken sind. Füge Milch und Butter langsam hinzu und zerdrücke die Kartoffeln mit einem Kartoffelstampfer. Rühre unter schwacher Hitze bis das Püree cremig ist. Schmecke es mit Salz und Muskat ab.

S. Stummreiter

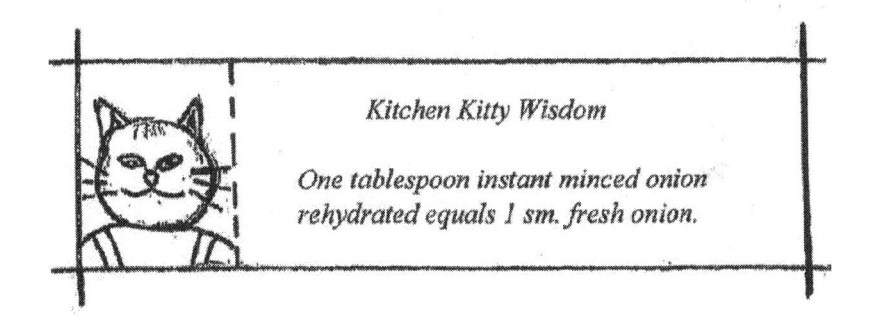

Kitchen Kitty Wisdom

One tablespoon instant minced onion rehydrated equals 1 sm. fresh onion.

Steinpilze in Rahm mit Breznknödel

500 g. Steinpilze
500 g. Brezen
500 ml. Milch, warm
6 Eier
1 Zwiebel
300 ml. Sahne
Knoblauch
Salz
Pfeffer
Kräuter
Muskat
Olivenöl

Soße:
Schneide die Zwiebel in kleine Stücke und schwitze sie in Olivenöl an. Schneide die Pilze in Scheiben und füge sie zur Pfanne hinzu. Kurz anbraten. Füge die Sahne hinzu und würze die Soße mit Salz, Pfeffer, Kräutern und Knoblauch. Lasse alles kurz köcheln.

Knödel:
Schneide die Brezen in kleine Stücke. Lege sie in eine Schüßel und füge die warme Milch hinzu. Füge die Eier hinzu und würze alles mit Salz, Pfeffer und Muskat. Mische alles gut durch. Forme aus der Maße eine Rolle und lege sie in ein Leinentuch. Binde die Enden zu und lege sie für ca. 35 min. in siedendes Waßer. Anschließend in dicke Scheiben schneiden und mit der Rahmsoße servieren.

Guten Appetit!

Xaver Stumreiter Family

Beilagen

Lauch – Kartoffel – Auflauf

500 g Lauch
750 g Kartoffeln
40 g Butter
25 g Mehl
Salz, Pfeffer
300 ml warme Milch
1 Prise geriebene Muskatnuss
50 g geriebener Emmentaler
Butter zum Einfetten

Lauch putzen und waschen. Das Grüne des Lauchs abschneiden und als Grundlage für die Brühe verwenden Soße 25 g Butter in einem Topf zerlaßen, Mehl einrühren und unter ständigem Rühren 2 Minuten darin hellbraun werden lassen. Vom Herd nehmen, Milch bis auf 2 EL unterrühren.

Wieder auf die Kochplatte zurückstellen und köcheln lassen, bis die Soße dick und glatt ist.
Nach und nach 150 ml Lauchbrühe unterrühren.
Nochmals aufkochen. Die weißen Teile des Lauchs in dicke Ringe schneiden, mit dem Grün 8 – 10 Minuten im Salz Waßer fast garkochen. Herausnehmen, abtropfen laßen, Flüßigkeit beiseite stellen.
Kartoffeln ca. 25 Minuten in Salz Waßer kochen.
Für die Kartoffeln in Scheiben schneiden, unter die weißen Lauchringe mischen.
In eine Form laßen, mit Salz, Pfeffer und Muskat abschmecken.
Ein Dritteln der füllen, Soße darüber gießen.

Restliche Kartoffeln pfeffern, mit 2 EL Milch und Butter zu Brei zerdrücken. Die Hälfte des Käses untermischen und abschmecken.

Kartoffelbrei über das Gemüse verteilen, den restlichen Käse darauf streuen.
20 – 25 Minuten im Backofen goldbraun backen.

Maria Haake

Alois und Maria Stumreiter

Marinierter Gemüsesalat

1 kleinen Kopf Blumenkohl
300 g. ganze grüne Bohnen
--or 250 g. Packung gefrorene grüne Bohnen
3 Karotten
2 kleine Zucchini
1 Taße frische, gehackte Petersilie

Vinaigrette Dreßing:

½ Taße Pflanzenöl
¼ Taße Apfelwein- oder Rotweinessig
3 Eßlöffel Zitronensaft
1 Teelöffel Worcestershire Soße
1 Teelöffel Salz
½ Teelöffel Senfpulver
½ Teelöffel grob gemahlenen schwarzen Pfeffer

Wasche und breche den Blumenkohlkopf in kleine mundgerechte Stücke. Wasche und schneide die grünen Bohnen oder taue die gefrorenen auf und gieße sie ab. Schäle und schneide die Karotten in dünne Streifen. Den Zucchini, die Petersilie und die grünen gefrorenen Bohnen müssen nicht gekocht werden. Blanchiere das folgende Gemüse separat: Blumenkohl – 6 min.; frische grüne Bohnen – 4 min.; Karotten – 3 min. Lege das Gemüse sofort in Eiswaßer, um den Kocheffekt zu stoppen. Trockne es gut in einem Sieb und lege es beiseite.
Bereite die Vinaigrette vor. Mische alle Zutaten für das Dressing in einem Einmachglas (Füllmenge: ½ l) und schüttel es, um es gut zu vermischen. Schichte das Gemüse in einer tiefen 3 Liter Glaßchüßel in folgender Reihenfolge: 1/3 des Blumenkohls, der Bohnen, der Karotten, der Zucchini und der frischen Petersilie. Füge die Vinaigrette während dem Schichten hinzu und wiederhole es weitere zwei Male. Mische es nicht zusammen. Bedecke es gut und kühle es über Nacht.

Ggfs. das Dreßing in eine andere Schüßel abgießen und erneut über dem Gemüse verteilen. Für 10 – 12 Personen. Dieser Salat kann in der Glaßchüßel oder auf einer Gemüseplatte mit Kopfsalatblättern serviert werden.

R. E. Westphal

Oma's „Reiberdatschi"

8 große Kartoffel
2 Eier
Salz
3 Eßlöffel
Butterschmalz zum Ausbacken
Die geschälten, rohen Kartoffeln reiben, gut abtropfen lassen oder leicht ausdrücken, die Eier und das Mehl unterrühren, salzen.
Mit einen Eßlöffel kleine „Reiberdatschi" in eine Pfanne mit heißem Fett setzen, hellbraun und knusprig auf beiden Seiten backen.
Dazu eignet sich am besten Apfelkompott oder auch Sauerkraut.

Katrin Mühlbauer (geborene Stumreiter)

Preiselbeer-Selleriesamen-Salatdressing

2/3 Taße Zucker
5 Eßlöffel Honig
1 Teßöffel Salz
1 Eßlöffel Zwiebeln
1 Esslöffel Selleriesamen
1 Teelöffel Paprika
1 Eßlöffel Zitronensaft
1 Eßlöffel Senfmehl
1/3 Taße Preiselbeer-Essig
½ Taße Waßer
¾ Taße Preiselbeeren
¾ Taße Salatöl

Mische den Eßig, das Waßer, die Preiselbeeren und die Zwiebeln im Mixer und mixe es kurz bei hoher Stufe. Kippe alles in einen Kochtopf und füge alle Zutaten hinzu, außer das Öl. Erhitze es und rühre bei mittlerer Heizung um bis sich der Zucker aufgelöst hat. Kippe alles in ein Einmachglas, füge das Öl hinzu und schüttel es gut durch. Kann vorab hergestellt und gekühlt werden. Paßt hervorragend zu Spinatsalat.
*Preiselbeer-Eßig:
1 Taße halbierte Preiselbeeren
2 Taßen Weißweinessig

Kippe alles in ein Einmachglas und laß es für 1 – 2 Wochen auf der Küchentheke stehen. Seihe alles durch einen Kaffeefilter oder ein Käsetuch. Benutze es für das o. g. Salatdreßing.

Bill Westphal

Bayrischer Obatzda

225 g. Brie Käse
30 g. Butter
2 EL Zwiebeln (fein gewürfelt)
2 EL Sauerrahm
¼ TL Paprikapulver, scharf
1 TL Paprikapulver, edelsüß
2 Msp. schwarzen Pfeffer, frisch gemahlen
1 Msp. Kümmel, gemahlen
¼ TL Meersalz
½ TL mittelscharfer Senf
30 ml. Helles / Lagerbier

Für die Dekoration: Schnittlauch und Zwiebelringe
Nehme den Brie aus dem Kühlschrank und schneide die Rinde ab. Schneide ihn in Stücke. Laße alle Zutaten Raumtemperatur erreichen. Zerdrücke alle Zutaten, außer den Schnittlauch, mit einer Gabel und vermenge alles. Dekoriere die Maße mit Schnittlauch und Zwiebelringen. Kalt servieren mit Brezen oder Brot.

S. Stummreiter

Stummreiter Family

Gurken mit Sauerrahm

1 Taße Sauerrahm
1 knappen Eßlöffel Zucker
2 Eßlöffel Apfelweineßig
¼ Taße gehackten, frischen Dill
¼ Teelöffel weißen Pfeffer
½ Teelöffel Salz
1 Teelöffel Selleriesamen
2 lange, schlanke Gurken
1 kleine Zwiebel
Gehackten, frischen Dill

Mische den Sauerrahm, den Zucker, den Eßig, den Dill, den Pfeffer, das Salz und die Selleriesamen in einer mittelgroßen Schüssel zusammen und vermenge alles gut. Schäle die Gurken und schneide sie so dünn wie möglich. Wasche die Zwiebel und schneide sie ein wenig dicker als die Gurken. Füge das Gemüse zur Sauerrahm-Mischung hinzu und schwenke es leicht. Kühle alles für mindestens 2 Stunden, damit die Gurken das Dreßing aufsaugen. Streue zusätzlichen Dill darüber und serviere es.

Bill Westphal

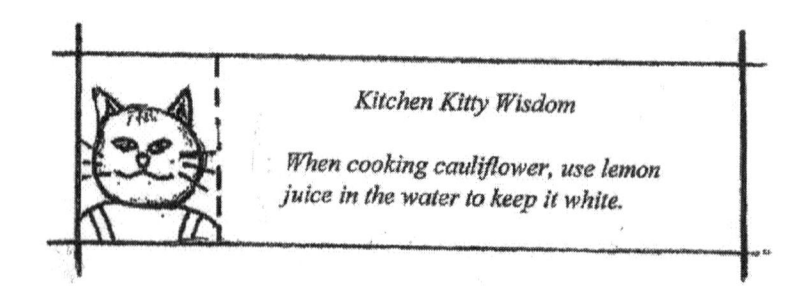

Kitchen Kitty Wisdom

When cooking cauliflower, use lemon juice in the water to keep it white.

Gurkengemüse in Buttersoße

1-1/2 kg. Gurken, Salz, Zitronensaft

zur Buttersoße:
30 gr. Butter
30 gr. Mehl
etwas Zwiebeln nach Belieben
1/4 ltr. Weißwein
3-4 Eßloeffel Sahne
Dill, Petersilie oder Tomatenmark

Gurken waschen, schälen, der Laenge nach halbieren, eventuell von Kernen befreien, in etwa kleinfingergroße Stuecke schneiden, nur leicht salzen, mit Zitronensaft beträufeln, etwas durchziehen laßen. Inzwischen helle Buttersoße herstellen, Gurken dazugeben und mit Weißwein aufgießen, bei mäßiger Hitze zugedeckt garen, ca.20-30 Minuten, zuletzt Sahne und kleingeschnittenen Dill oder Petersilie oder Tomatenmark nach Geschmack beifügen, abschmecken, nicht mehr kochen laßen. Mir gekochten Kartoffeln oder Reis servieren.

Rita Stumreiter

Heißes Tomatenbrot nach Cajun-Art

1 Taße Bloody Mary Mix (Tabasco)
1 Taße Waßer
1 Packung aktive Trockenhefe
1/3 Taße Honig
¼ Taße Pflanzenöl
¼ Taße gehacktes Zwiebelgrün
¼ Taße gehackte Petersilie
1 Knoblauchzehe, gepreßt
1 Teelöffel Salz
5 bis 6 Taßen Haushaltsmehl

Mische den Bloody Mary Mix und das Waßer in einem Kochtopf. Koche es bei niedriger Flamme bis die Mischung 40 °C erreicht hat. Kippe es dann in eine große, warme Schüßel. Füge die Hefe hinzu. Rühre bis sie sich aufgelöst hat. Füge den Honig, das Öl, das Zwiebelgrün, die Petersilie, den Knoblauch und das Salz hinzu und vermische es gut. Füge 1 Taße Mehl hinzu und rühre es glatt. Füge nach und nach das restliche Mehl hinzu bis sich ein fester Teig gebildet hat. Knete den Teig auf einem leicht bemehlten Untergrund für 5 Minuten oder bis er glatt und elastisch ist. Forme den Teig zu einer Kugel. Lege ihn in eine eingefettete, große Schüßel. Bedecke die Schüßel und stelle sie für 1 Stunde an einen warmen Platz, damit der Teig aufgehen kann bzw. laße ihn dort stehen bis er seine Größe erreicht hat.

Drücke die Luft aus dem aufgegangenen Teig und teile ihn in zwei gleichgroße Stücke. Rolle beide Stücke auf bemehltem Untergrund jeweils zu einem Rechteck aus. Rolle jedes Stück von der kürzeren Seite aus dicht wie eine Biskuitrolle ein. Drücke die Enden ein, um die Rolle zu versiegeln. Lege sie in eine Kastenform mit den Maßen 23 x 13 x 8 cm. Bedecke die Kastenform und stelle sie an einen warmen Platz, damit sie der Teig eine weitere Stunde aufgehen kann bzw. laße ihn dort stehen bis er seine Größe erreicht hat.

Backe den Teig in einem vorheizten Ofen bei 200 °C für etwa 30 min. oder bis der Laib sich hohl anhört, wenn man draufklopft und die Kruste braun ist. Nehme den Laib aus der Form und kühle ihn auf dem Rost. Rezept für 2 Laibe

R. E. Westphal

Bloody Mary Mix

Oma's Reiberdatschi mit Apfelkompott

Reiberdatschi:
1 kg. Kartoffeln, mehlig kochend
1 Zwiebel
3 Eier
1 Prise Salz
2 EL Mehl
Rapsöl
Apfelkompott:
800 g. Äpfel
1 EL Zitronensaft
250 ml. Waßer
2 EL Zucker
½ TL Zimt

Reiberdatschi:
Schäle die Kartoffeln und reibe sie fein. Lege die Raspeln auf ein Küchentuch und drücke die Stärke heraus. Schneide die Zwiebeln in klein und füge sie zu den geriebenen Kartoffeln hinzu. Rühre die Eier, das Salz und das Mehl unter. Erhitze das Öl in einer Pfanne, forme flache Pfannkuchen aus den geriebenen Kartoffeln und brate sie knusprig.

Apfelkompott:
Gebe den Zitronensaft und das Waßer in eine Schüßel. Wasche, schäle, viertel und entkerne die Äpfel. Schneide sie in Scheiben und gebe sie ins Zitronenwaßer. Füge den Zucker hinzu und koche alles bei mittlerer Hitze für 15 – 20 min. Garniere das Kompott mit Zimt. Serviere es warm oder kalt.
Für 3 Personen.

S. Stummreiter

Rosenkohltopf

400 gr. Paprikawurst
3 Eßloeffel Butter oder Oel
2 Zwiebeln
500 gr. Rosenkohl
4 Kartoffeln
1 ltr. Fleischbruehe
1 Knoblauchzehe
1 Teeloeffel Salz
1 Eßloeffel Paprika
1Meßerspitze Muskat
1 Prise Zucker
Salz, Pfeffer
1 Becher Saure Sahne
1 Bund Liebstoeckel

Paprikawurst in Wuerfel schneiden, im Topf Butter oder Oel geben und die Wurst anbraten, Zwiebeln dazugeben, dann kleingewürfelte Kartoffeln und dann geputzten Rosenkohl, kurz durchkochen, Fleischbruehe aufgießen und ca.30 min bei mittlerer Hitze köcheln lassen, Knoblauchzehe mit Salz gut zerreiben, mit der Knoblauchzehe, Paprika, Muskat und Zucker würzen, mit Salz und Pfeffer abschmecken. Vom Herd nehmen, saure Sahne unterziehen und mit gehacktem Liebstoeckel bestreuen.

Rita Stumreiter

Sellerieschnitzel

1 kg. Sellerie-mittelgroße Knolle
Salz
Zitronensaft
Zum Panieren:
3-4 Eßloeffel Mehl
2 Eier mit 1 Teel. Oel und 2 Eßloeffel Waßer verschlagen
8-10 Eßloeffel Semmelbroesel

Oel oder anderes Backfett, Zitronenspalten, Petersilie
Sellerie waschen, in Waßer gründlich bürsten, schälen, nochmal waschen, In gut 1/2 cm dicke Scheiben schneiden, diese leicht salzen, mit Zitronensaft beträufeln, etwa 1 Stunde durchziehen laßen, erst in Mehl wenden, dann in Eimischung geben und dann in Semmelbroesel wenden, in heißem Oel auf beiden Seiten langsam goldbraun backen, so daß der Sellerie in dieser Zeit weich wird. Backzeit etwa 10-15 Minuten. Mit Zitronenspalten und Petersiliengruen anrichten, mit Kartoffelsalat und grünem Salat zu Tisch geben.

Rita Stumreiter

Sellerieschnitzel

Tante Catherine's Limonen-Götterspeise-Salat

1 Packung Limonen-Götterspeise, aufgelöst in einer ¾ vollen Taße mit kochendem Waßer, abkühlen laßen
1 Taße Schlagsahne
1 Taße abgetropften Obstsalat aus der Dose oder anderes Dosenobst, in kleine Stücke vorgeschnitten
1 Taße Hüttenkäse
½ Taße gehackte Nüße, wenn gewünscht

Mische alle Zutaten zusammen. Kippe die Götterspeise in eine Gußform, bevor sie sich verfestigt, wenn gewünscht. Schmeckt am besten, wenn sie über Nacht zieht.

R. E. Westphal

Weißbierkiachal

600 gr. Mehl
2 Eier
80 gr. Zucker
1 Prise Salz
2 Paeckchen Backpulver
1 x Hefeweißbier 0,5 lt.

Alles in eine Schueßel geben und verrühren. Mit einem Teeloeffel abstechen und in schwimmenden heißem Fett hell backen.

Maria Haake

Nachspeisen

Altmodische Haferflockenkekse

1 Taße Rosinen
¾ Taße Backfett
2 Eier
2 ½ Taßen Mehl
1 Teelöffel Natron
1 Teelöffel Zimt
2 Taßen kernige Haferflocken
1 Taße Waßer
1 ½ Taßen Zucker
1 Teelöffel Vanille
½ Teelöffel Backpulver
1 Teelöffel Salz
½ Teelöffel Nelken
½ Taße gehackte Nüße

Bei geringer Hitze die Rosinen und das Waßer in einem Kochtopf 20 – 30 min. kochen bis sie voll sind. Die Rosinenflüssigkeit in einem Meßbecher abgießen. Füge genügend Waßer hinzu, um daraus eine ½ Taße zu machen.

Heize den Ofen auf 200 °C vor. Mische das Backfett, den Zucker, die Eier und die Vanille zusammen. Rühre die Rosinenflüßigkeit unter. Mische die trockenen Zutaten unter. Füge die Haferflocken, die Rosinen und die Nüße hinzu. Tröpfle den Teig von einem runden Teelöffel im Abstand von 5 cm auf ein ungefettetes Backpapier. Backe alles für 8 – 10 min. oder bis die Kekse leicht angebräunt sind.

R. E. Westphal

Bay Pfannkuchen

250 gr. Mehl
3 Eier
1/2 l. Mich
1 Prise Salz
Backfett

Mehl mit Milch und Eier und Salz zu einem glatten,dünnen Teig verrühren, 1/2 Std. stehen laßen, in der Pfanne 1 Eßloeffel Fett erhitzen, den Boden dünn mit Teig bedecken(Pfanne anheben damit der Teig verlaufen kann), auf beiden Seiten goldgelb backen.
Man kann die Pfannkuchen nach Belieben mit Marmelade, Zucker, Honig, Eiscreme, oder mit Gemuese, Pilzen, Hackfleisch, Salat füllen und aufrollen oder Pfannkuchen noch heiß aufrollen und erkalten laßen, klein schneiden und in eine Fleisch-Gemuesebruehe geben, Schnittlauch darüber streuen.

Rita Stumreiter

Pfannkuchen

Bayrisch Creme

4 Eigelb,
75-100 gr. Zucker
1 Vanillestange,
1/4 l. Milch
6 Blatt Gelatine
1/2 l. Schlagrahm

Eigelb mit Zucker schaumig rühren, die kalte Milch und geklopfte, gespaltene Vanillestange dazugeben, am Feuer abschlagen bis die Maße dick ist(nicht kochen). Gelatine in kaltem Waßer einweichen, ausdrücken, in der heißen Creme auflösen, umrühren, kalt stellen. Wenn die Creme zu stocken beginnt, den steifen Schlagrahm unterziehen, in kalt ausgespülte Form füllen, kalt stellen.
Ich teile immer die Maße und gebe in die eine Haelfte immer Schokolade, oder Nugatcreme oder Sirup. Die Creme verwende ich oft in Verbindung mit Angel Cake und variiere nach Saison mit Fruechten.

Rita Stumreiter

Bayerische Creme

Gewürzkuchen

175 gr. Butter
4 Eier getrennt
300 gr. Zucker
1 Teel.Zimt
1/2 Teel.Nelken
50 gr. Kakao
1/8-1/4 l. Milch
375 gr. Mehl
1 P.Backpulver
4 Eßl.saeuerliche Marmelade
Puderzucker

Butter schaumig rühren, Eigelb und Zucker abwechselnd dazugeben und schaumig rühren, Mehl, Gewuerze und soviel Milch zugeben, daß der Teig breit und schwer vom Loeffel fällt.Zuletzt den Eischnee unterheben. In vorbereitete Springform füllen, bei 175-200 C eine Stunde backen. Am nächsten Tag einmal durchschneiden, mit Marmelade fuellen, mit Puderzucker bestreuen.
Man kann 100 gr. gemahlene Nüße unter den Teig mischen.

Rita Stumreiter

Gewürzkuchen

Grießschnitten

1 l. Milch
1 Prise Salz
1 Stückchen Zitronenschale
250 g. Grieß
30 g. Zucker
2-3 Eier

Zum Panieren nach Belieben:
1-2 Eier mit 1 EL Waßer verschlagen
6-8 EL Semmelbrösel mit 2 EL Mehl gemischt
Backfett
Zucker und Zimt

Sehr steifen Grießbrei kochen, noch heiß Zucker und Eier unterrühren
Sofort auf naßem Brett 1 cm. dick außtreichen oder Maße in kalt gespülter Kastenform ausdrücken, völlig erkalten laßen.
Aus der erkalteten Maße Schnitten schneiden (Kastenform dazu stürzen)
Schnitten in heißen Fett auf Stielpfanne auf beiden Seiten goldgelb backen
Nach Belieben vor dem Backen panieren
Auf heißer Platte anrichten und nach Belieben mit Zucker-Zimtmischung bestreuen
Nicht paniert sind die Schnitten weniger fettreich und deshalb bekömmlicher
Grießschnitten ohne Zucker können als selbständiges Gericht mit Salat serviert warden.

Maria Haake

Linzer Sternchen

200 gr. Mehl, 200 gr. Butter
100 gr. Zucker
100 gr. gem.Mandeln
1/2 Teel.Zimt
1 Prise Nelken und Kardamon
Rote Marmalade zum Fuellen
Puderzucker

Aus Mehl, Butter, Zucker, gem. Mandeln, Zimt, Nelken, Kardamon gebröselten Muerbteig herstellen, mind. 2 Std. kalt stellen. Den Teig meßerrueckendick auswellen, Sternchen außtechen. Die Haelfte der Sternchen in der Mitte mit einem runden Loch versehen. Die Plaetzchen nochmals kalt stellen, bei 180-195 C. hellgelb backen. Je ein gelochtes und ein ungelochtes Sternchen werden mit roter Marmelade so zusammengesetzt, daß die Zacken der Sternchen versetzt aufeinander liegen. Die Oberseite mit Puderzucker bestreuen.

Rita Stumreiter

Linzer Sternchen

Mama's mit Datteln gefüllte Zuckerkekse

Dattelfüllung:
1 Packung gehackte Datteln
½ Dose Kondensmilch
1 Eßlöffel Zucker

Mische alle Zutaten in einem Kochtopf zusammen und erhitze es unter ständigem Rühren auf mittlerer Stufe bis die Mischung dickflüßig ist und sprudelt. Nehme den Topf vom Herd und laße es abkühlen.

Keksteig:
¾ Taße Backfett
1 Taße gekörnten Zucker
2 Eier
½ Teelöffel Vanillearoma
½ Teelöffel Zitronenaroma
2 ½ Taßen Mehl
1 Teelöffel Backpulver
1 Teelöffel Salz

Heize den Ofen auf 200 °C vor. Mische das Backfett, den gekörnten Zucker, die Eier und die Aromastoffe gut zusammen. Mische dann das Mehl, das Backpulver und das Salz unter. Bedecke und kühle es für 1 Stunde. Rolle den Teig 0,3 cm dick auf einer leicht bemehlten Fläche aus. Schneide kleine Kreise in Größe eines kleinen Donuts aus. Vor dem Backen jeweils zwei Kekse mit 1 Teelöffel Dattelmischung in der Mitte aufeinanderlegen (im Sandwich-Stil). Drücke die Ränder mit Gabelzinken ein. Backe alles für 8 min. oder bis die Ränder leicht angebräunt sind. Reicht für ca. 24 Stück.

R. E. Westphal

Riegel aus Apfel-Plundergebäck

2 ½ Taßen Mehl
1 Teelöffel Salz
1 Taße Backfett
1 Taße Zucker
1 Teelöffel Zimt
1 Eiweiß
8 – 10 mittelgroße Äpfel
1 Eigelb + 2/3 Taße Milch
1 Taße geschrotete Cornflakes-Cerealien

Mische das Backfett in Mehl und Salz. Füge die Milch-Eigelb-Mischung hinzu. Vermische es mit einer Gabel. Rolle die Hälfte des Teigs in ein Backblech der Größe 26 x 40 cm. Bestreue den.

Teig mit den Cornflakes. Schäle und schneide die Äpfel in dünne Scheiben. Lege sie über den Teig mit den Cornflakes. Bestreue alles mit Zucker und Zimt. Rolle die andere Hälfte des Teigs aus und lege sie oben drauf. Drücke die Ränder zusammen. Schlage das Eiweiß und bestreiche damit die zweite Teighälfte. Backe es für 60 Minuten bei 200 °C.

Glasur:
1 Taße Puderzucker
1 Eßlöffel Waßer
½ Teelöffel Vanille

Mische alle Zutaten zusammen. Wenn die Maße zu dick ist, füge ein wenig mehr Waßer hinzu.

R. E. Westphal

Schokoladensplitter-Dattel-Kuchen

Mische 1 Taße gehackte Dattel, 1 Teelöffel Natron und 1 ½ Taßen kochendes Waßer und laß es abkühlen.
Schlage ½ Taße Backfett mit 1 Taße Zucker schaumig. Füge 2 gut verrührte Eier hinzu. Rühre alles gut zusammen und füge die Dattel-Mischung hinzu.
Siebe 1 ¼ Taßen + 3 Eßlöffel Mehl und ¾ Teelöffel Natron zusammen.
Mische es mit o. g. Mischung zusammen. Vermische alles gut und kippe es in eine 23 x 33 cm große gefettete und bemehlte Pfanne.

Füge folgende Toppings vor dem Backen hinzu:

30 – 170 Gramm Packung Schokoladensplitter
½ Taße Zucker
½ Taße gehackte Nüße

Vermische alles und streue es oben drauf. Backe es für 45 Minuten bei 175 °C.

R. E. Westphal

Schokoladensplitter-Dattel-Kuchen

Elisenlebkuchen

5 Eier
500 gr. Zucker
500 gr. gemahlene Mandeln oder Haselnuese
 oder gemischt
100 gr. Zitronat
100 gr. Orangat
2 abgetriebene Zitronenschalen
1 Teel.Zimt
1/2 Teel.Ginger
1 Meßerspitze Nelken
Kardamon

Eier und Zucker schaumig ruehren(mind,15 min.), kleingeschnittenes Zitronat und Orangat, abgetriebene Zitronenschale, Zimt, Nelken, Kardamom, Ginger und Nueße dazugeben(die Menge der Nuesse richtet sich nach der Eigroeße, der Teig soll noch streichfähig bleiben), die Maße auf runde Oblaten streichen(Rand frei laßen,da der Teig beim Backen etwas auseinanderläuft), auf gewachstes Backblech legen. Bei 150-160 C langsam backen. Die Lebkuchen noch warm mit Glasur oder Kuvertuere überziehen.

Rita Stumreiter

Kaiserschmarrn

250 gr. Mehl
1 priese Salz
375 ml. Milch
4 Eier
3 Eßlöffel Zucker
2 Eßlöffel Butter
100 gr. Sultaninen

Mehl, Salz, Milch, Eigelb und Zucker verrühren.
Eiweiß zu steifen Schnee schlagen und unter den Teig heben.
Fett in die Pfanne geben und einen Teil des Teig hineingießen.
Sultaninen daraufstreuen, langsam braten.
Wenden und fertig braten. Mit restlichen Teig so weiter...

Liz Kaupp

Blaubeereis mit Joghurt

200 gr. Blaubeeren
300 ml. Naturjoghurt
300 ml. Sahne
120 gr. Zucker
Saft von 1 Zitrone

Blaubeeren waschen und zu einer Creme pueriren, Zucker, Zitronensaft hinzufügen.

Danach vermischen Sie alles mit der Sahne und dem Joghurt und füllen die Menge in die Eismaschine.

Maria Haake

Bananen-Nuß-Brot

1 Taße Zucker
½ Taße Backfett
2 Eier
1 Teelöffel Natron
2 Taßen Mehl
½ Taße gehackte Nüße
1 Meßerspitze Salz
3 Bananen, zerdrückt

Heize den Ofen auf 175 °C vor. Fette eine Kastenform mit der Größe 23 cm x 13 cm ein.
Kombiniere den Zucker und das Backfett und mische es gut durch.
Füge die Eier hinzu und rühre sie langsam unter. Füge dann die zerdrückten Bananen hinzu.
Füge die Mehl- und Natronmixtur hinzu und rühre bis der Teig gut durchgemischt ist.
Löffle alles in die Kastenform und backe es bei 40 – 60 Minuten bzw. bis es durch ist.
Reicht für 1 Laib Brot.

R. E. Westphal

Bill's Pflaumenlikör

Wasche und trockne etwa 2 ½ Meßbecher kleine italienische Pflaumen.

Fülle alles in Einmachgläser.

Rechne pro Liter eine ¾ Taße Zucker und gebe ihn zu den Pflaumen.

Füge 1 Liter Gin hinzu.

Verschließe die Einmachgläser zusammen mit dem Gummiring.

Schüttle die Einmachgläser einmal am Tag bis sich der Zucker aufgelöst hat.

Das Getränk ist 3 Monate nach Herstellung fertig. Guten Genuß!

Hinweis: Es können auch andere Früchte benutzt werden – sei kreativ!

Bill Westphal

Holländische Mandelkekse

225 gr. Mehl
1 Eigelb
150 gr. Sauerrahm
75 gr. Zucker
1 Paeckchen Orangenaroma
100 gr. Butter
Außerdem:
100 gr. Orangenmarmelade
200 gr. Mandelplaettchen

Mehl auf Arbeitsfläche sieben, Mulde eindrücken, Eigelb und Sauerrahm in die Mulde geben, Zucker und Orangenaroma darüber streuen, die kalte Butter in kl. Stueckchen dazugeben. Das ganze mit den Haenden von außen nach innen schnell zu einem glatten, kompakten Teig verkneten. Den Muerbteig in Folie wickeln und im Kuehlschrank mindestens 1 Stunde ruhen laßen. Anschließend den Teig 1/2 cm dick ausrollen und runde Plaetzchen außtechen, diese auf ein mit Backpapier belegtes Backblech setzen und im auf 180 C vorgeheizten Backofen etwa 10 min backen. Die fertigen Plaetzchen auf einem Kuchengitter erkalten laßen. Die Orangenmarmalade aufkochen, durch ein Sieb streichen, die Plaetzchen damit bestreichen und in die Mandelblaettchen tauchen. Nach dem abtrocknen in einer Dose kühl lagern.

Maria Haake

Orangenkuchen, Zitronenkuchen

200 gr. Butter
200-250 gr. Zucker
4 ganze Eier
Schale von 2 Bioorangen bzw. Zitronen
2 Eßloeffel Milch nach Bedarf
250 gr. Mehl,
125 gr. Speisestaerke
1/2 Paeckchen Backpulver

zur Form: Butter und Mehl
evtl. zum Traenken: Saft von 2-3 Orangen und 1 Zitrone
Aprikosenmarmelade
Orangen- oder Zitronenglasur:
200-250 gr. Puderzucker
2 Eßloeffel Zitronen-oder Orangensaft
1-2 Eßloeffel warmes Waßer nach Bedarf oder 1/2-1. Eiklar

Sehr lockere Schaummaße rühren aus Butter, Zucker und ganzen Eiern, fein abgeriebene Orangen-oder Zitronenschale unterrühren, Mehl mit Staerkemehl und Backpulver gemischt und gesiebt, im Wechsel mit wenig Milch (nach Bedarf) hinzugeben, Teig muß breit und schwer vom Loeffel reißend fallen.Teig in gut gebutterte und bemehlte Kastenform geben, glatt streichen, bei mäßiger Mittelhitze (180-190 C) 1 Stunde backen, in der Form etwas abkühlen laßen, dann stürzen.

Den abgkuehlten Kuchen nach Belieben mit einem spitzen Hoelzchen mehrmals einstechen, mit Orangen-Zitronensaft vorsichtig beträufeln, Saft jeweils gut einziehen laßen, mit Glasur überziehen; oder den erkälteten Kuchen mit Aprikosenmarmelade dünn bestreichen und dann glasieren.Man kann den kalten Kuchen auch einmal durchschneiden, traenken, mit Marmelade füllen, zusammensetzen, mit Marmelade dünn bestreichen und glasieren.

Maria Haake

Rote Gruetze

750 gr. Beerenfruechte (Johannisbeere, Blaubeere, Erdbeere, Himbeere, Brombeere)
100-150 gr. Zucker
Saft und Schale von 1 Biozitrone
2-3 Teeloeffel Staerkemehl
1/2 ltr. Kirschsaft

Beeren waschen und in einem großen Topf geben, Zucker und Zitronensaft dazugeben und mit Kirschsaft auffüllen und nur 1mal kurz aufkochen, zur Seite stellen, Staerke mit etwas Zucker und Waßer anrühren und in die Beerenmaße einrühren, die Himbeeren erst jetzt dazugeben, nochmal kurz aufkochen und dann in Desertschalen abfüllen. Mit Sahne und Fruechten servieren.

Franzi Sweekhorst/Stumreiter

Scheiterhaufen

8 alte Semmeln oder Croißant (2Tage)
etwa 3/4 ltr. Milch
1 Prise Salz, Zitronenschale
60-80 gr. Zucker,
2-3 Eier
3/4 - 1 kg. saftige Aepfel oder Kirschen oder Zwetschgen
50 gr. Rosinen (b.Aepfeln)
100 gr. Nueße
Zum Backen: 30 gr. Butter

Semmeln oder Croißant in ca.1 cm. dicke Scheiben schneiden; Milch, Salz, abgeriebene Zitronenschale, Zucker und Eier gut verquirlen, über geschnittene Semmeln gießen, durchziehen laßen. Aepfel schälen, in feine Scheiben schneiden oder Kirschen bzw. Zwetschgen waschen und entsteinen; Weinbeeren waschen, brühen, abtropfen laßen. In gefettete Auflaufform abwechselnd eine Lage eingeweichte Semmeln/Croißant, eine Lage vorbereitetes Obst und Rosinen geben, oberste Lage Semmeln/Croißant; oder Semmel/Croißantmaße mit Obst gemischt einfüllen, mit Gehackten Nueßen bestreuen. Rest der Eiermilch darüber gießen, mit Butterflocken belegen, im vorgeheiztem Backofen etwa 1/2 - 3/4 Stunde backen.

Maria Haake

Schneefloeckchen

4 Eiweiß
200 gr. feinen Zucker
1 gehäufter Teeloeffel Speisestaerke
1/2 Teeloeffel Anispulver

Die Eiweiße in eine saubere Schueßel geben und steif schlagen. Den Zucker mit der Speisestaerke und dem Anispulver vermischen und langsam unter den Eischnee schlagen. Die Maße in einen Spritzbeutel mit Lochtuelle füllen und kleine Haeufchen auf ein mit Backpapier belegtes Backblech spritzen. Die Baisers im auf 120 C vorgeheizten Backofen 1 1/2 Std. mehr trocknen als backen. Die fertigen Plaetzchen aus dem Ofen nehmen und auskühlen laßen. In einer Dose kühl aufbewahren.

Rita Stumreiter

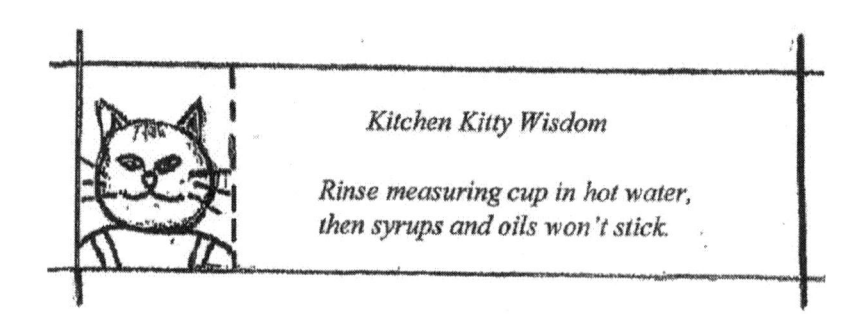

Kitchen Kitty Wisdom

Rinse measuring cup in hot water, then syrups and oils won't stick.

Schokoladenkuchen (Abruzzen)

100 gr. geschälte Mandeln
200 gr. Schokoladenkuvertuere
5 Eier
80 gr Butter + 1 El fuer die Form
100 gr. Zucker
100 gr. Mehl
2 El Speisestaerke

5 Eier trennen, die 5 Eigelb mit Zucker schaumig schlagen, die Butter in einem Toepfchen zerlaßen, Mehl und Speisestaerke mischen, abwechselnd mit den gemahlenen Mandeln löffelweise unter den Eierschaum rühren, die flüssige und abgekühlte Butter ebenfalls unter den Teig mischen, Eiweiß zu steifen Schnee schlagen, gründlich und gleichmaeßig unter den Teig ziehen, Teigmaße in die gebutterte Springform geben und in den vorgeheizten Backofen bei 200° C backen, nach 25 min. die Oberflaeche des Kuchens mit Alufolie abdecken, in weiteren 10 min. fertig backen, aus dem Ofen nehmen, aus der Form lösen und abkühlen laßen ca 1 Std., die Schokoladenkuvertuere schmelzen und damit den Kuchen gleichmaeßig überziehen, mit einer Gabel feine Rillen als Muster einziehen.

Rita Stumreiter

Zitronen-Gugelhupf

220 gr. Mehl
45 gr. Staerkemehl
5 gr. Backpulver
245 gr. weiche Butter
140 gr. Puderzucker
1 Paeckchen Vanillezucker
8 Eidotter
2-3 abgeriebene Bio-Zitronenschale
8 Eiklar
100 gr. Zucker
1 Prise Salz
Zitronenglasur:
60-100 gr. Puderzucker
2-3 Eßloeffel frisch gepreßten Zitronensaft

Mehl mit Staerke und Backpulver sieben, weiche Butter mit Puderzucker schaumig schlagen, dann Vanillezucker und Zitronenschale dazugeben und die Eidotter nach und nach unterrühren. Anschliessend Eiklar mit Zucker und Salz zu cremigem Schnee schlagen und diesen unter die Dottermaße arbeiten. Danach das Mehlgemisch unterheben.

Die Teigmaße in eine gebutterte und bemehlte Gugelhupfform oder kleine Formen füllen und im vorgeheizten Backofen bei 160-170 C backen, kleine Formen ca.20 min., große Form bis zu 50 min,mit Holzstaebchen testen, den Gugelhupf nach dem Backen stürzen und vollständig auskühlen laßen.
Zitronenglasur herstellen-viel Puderzucker ergibt eine feste Glasur, wenig Puderzucker eine flüßigere, die Glasur auf dem Kuchen bzw. kleine Formen verteilen.

Rita Stumreiter

Der Kolmsteiner Hof

Familie Stumreiter
Kolmstein Kreuzwegstr. 9
93453 Neukirchen b. Hl. Blut
Tel. 09947-444
infor@kolmsteiner-hof.de
www.kolmsteiner-hof.de

The Kolmsteiner Hof

The restaurant and hotel, Kolmsteiner Hof near the town of Neukirchen beim Heilgen Blut in Bavaria is located amid the beautiful Bohemian Forest overlooking mountain ranges in the area.

The Kolmsteiner Hof was originally a rectory for the priest serving the nearby Catholic Church dedicated to the Virgin Mary.

In 1973 Xaver and Anna Stumreiter bought the priest house and renovated it into a restaurant and hotel. Guests are welcome for a meal, a night's stay, or after a long hike on one of the many trails through the forest. Customers enjoy the delicious meals prepared with ingredients picked fresh from the forest when in season, and relax in their private hotel rooms offering many amenities.

In 2004 Xaver's son, Alexander Stumreiter and his wife, Claudia became the new proprietors. Dining and being an overnight guest at this country inn is a delightful experience. When visiting in Bavaria, make this your home away from home. Visit them on their website at www.kolmsteiner-hof.de. An English translation is available.

Xaver has shared a recipe of one of their signature dishes at the restaurant. It can be found on page 116.

Der Kolmsteiner Hof

Das Restaurant und Hotel Kolmsteiner Hof nahe dem Ort Neukirchen beim Heilgen Blut in Bayern liegt inmitten des schönen Böhmerwaldes mit Blick auf die Bergketten der Umgebung.

Der Kolmsteiner Hof war ursprünglich ein Pfarrhaus für den Pfarrer der nahe gelegenen katholischen Kirche, die der Jungfrau Maria geweiht war.

1973 kauften Xaver und Anna Stumreiter das Pfarrhaus und bauten es zu einem Restaurant und Hotel um. Gäste sind willkommen für eine Mahlzeit, eine Nacht oder nach einer langen Wanderung auf einem der vielen Wege durch den Wald. Kunden genießen die köstlichen Mahlzeiten, die in der Saison mit frischen Zutaten aus der Umgebung zubereitet werden, und entspannen in ihren privaten Hotelzimmern mit vielen Annehmlichkeiten.

2004 wurden Xaver's Sohn Alexander Stumreiter und seine Frau Claudia die neuen Besitzer. Essen und Übernachten in diesem Landgasthof ist eine herrliche Erfahrung. Wenn Sie nach Bayern kommen, machen Sie es zu Ihrem Zuhause fern von Zuhause. Besuchen Sie sie auf ihrer Website unter www.kolmsteiner-hof.de. Eine englische Übersetzung ist verfügbar.

ADENDUM

Wild Rice Hot Dish

2 cups wild rice
1 can mushroom soup
1 small jar of mushrooms
2 tbsp. soy sauce
2 cans chicken rice soup
7 sticks celery
½ green pepper
1 onion
1 ½ lbs. ground beef
½ lb. pork sausage
1 tbsp. salt

Dice and boil celery and green pepper until soft. Dice and fry one onion. Fry ground beef and pork sausage. Mix all ingredients together and bake in 350 degrees oven for one hour. (Soak wild rice for 24 hours to soften before mixing).

Pam Bartoe

Catherine Stumreiter Mabie's Rhubarb Jam

4 cups washed and cut up rhubarb
4 cups sugar
1/4 cup water
Combine and cook for 15 minutes.
Add: 1- 3oz. pkg. strawberry gelatin and stir to dissolve gelatin.
Pour into sterilized jars to within ¼ inch of top. Put on lid, screw band firmly tight. Process in Boiling Water Bath 10 minutes. Take jars from water and place on rack to cool.
Note: Jam will be soft.

Ginger and Sherb Mabie

Grandma Amelia's kitchen stove

Gelatin-Carrot-Pineapple Salad

1-3oz. pkg. lime or lemon flavored gelatin
1 sm. can crushed pineapple; strain and reserve liquid
1-1/2 cups grated fresh carrots
1/3 cup finely diced celery
Mix gelatin with one cup boiling water and stir until dissolved. Measure pineapple liquid and add cold water to make ¾ cup. Stir into dissolved gelatin. Stir in crushed pineapple, carrots and celery. Pour into medium sized mold. Refrigerate until firmly set. Serve with optional Mayo dressing.

Mayo Dressing:
½ cup Mayonnaise
1 tsp. sugar
Stir in cream until dressing is of desired consistency. Serve with gelatin salad.

Duane Mabie's Favorite

R. Elaine Westphal

Ryan's Special Brownies

With the legalization of Cannabis in California in 2018, most people now buy "edibles" (i.e. THC infused food products) at their local Cannabis Dispensary. However, long before recreational legalization many people made their own edibles, enjoying the benefits of Cannabis without the downsides of smoking. This particular recipe has received rave reviews - the brownies have hardly any Cannabis flavor - so watch out and keep out of reach of children!

Ghirardelli Dark Chocolate Brownie Mix is widely available, and a personal favorite of mine; however, any oil based brownie mix will work fine. We'll also be using a 13x9 baking dish instead of the recommended 8x8, simply because it's a bit easier to portion sizes when the brownies are a bit thinner.

IMPORTANT NOTE: While Cannabis is generally non-toxic, eating too much can lead to uncomfortable side effects such as nausea and disorientation and, in some cases, uncomfortable mental states such as paranoia. As with any mind altering substance (such as Alcohol), you should not plan to drive or perform any tasks requiring fine motor skills. When trying Cannabis Edibles for the first time, take a very small portion (such as 1/4 of a brownie in this recipe) and wait 60-90 minutes to evaluate the effects before trying more. If you do find yourself taking too much, simply lie down in a quiet dark room and wait for the THC to leave your system - though this may take several hours.

Ingredients:
1 Box of Brownie Mix (Oil Based, not Butter)
I like: http://www.directionsforme.org/item/3271974
1 Cone Coffee filter (can sub folded cheese cloth)

1 16 oz measuring cup or small bowl
1/4 cup water
1/2 cup of olive or canola oil
1 egg
1/3 ounce of Cannabis Flower (I recommend a Sativa strain like Super Silver Haze)

1/2 Tbs of Butter

Equipment:
Double boiler pot
Spice scale (to weigh Cannabis Flower)
Wooden Spoon
Spice Grinder or small Food Processor
Mixing Bowl
13"x9" baking pan

Instructions:
Cannabis Infused Oil:

The goal here is to gently heat the oil and Cannabis mix at a temperature between 175° F and 250° F. A double boiler works perfectly for this. Add water to bottom boiler pot, then warm 1/2 cup of oil on medium heat in the double boiler pot. Coarsely grind the 1/3 oz of Cannabis flower, and add to pot, stirring to mix with the oil. Let the oil cook for 3-5 hours, stirring occasionally and adjusting burner temperature to keep water boiling but not evaporating too quickly. Use fan on cook top to limit the odor of the oil or open windows in the kitchen. Be sure to check and re-fill water in bottom boiler pot as needed so oil does not over heat.

When Cannabis has infused into oil, let cool and then strain through coffee filter (or cheese cloth) into measuring cup or small bowl. Use wooden spoon to help push oil though. You will end up with a little over 1/3 cup of infused oil, as some oil will be left with the flower, discard flower and filter.

Brownie Mix:

Follow the directions on the box, using the Cannabis infused oil:
Preheat oven to 325 degrees F. Prepare baking pan by lightly greasing with butter. Place water, oil and egg in mixing bowl and stir until fully mixed. Add brownie mix and stir until well blended. Spread in prepared pan and bake for 25-35 minutes. Do not over bake.

Cool completely in pan before cutting. Cut into 24 brownies, which can be refrigerated or frozen to store.

Enjoy the brownies (remember to try with about 1/4 a brownie to start) while relaxing and listening to your favorite music or a movie!

Ryan Lewis (Mary Jo Stumreiter Lewis Nickum's Son)

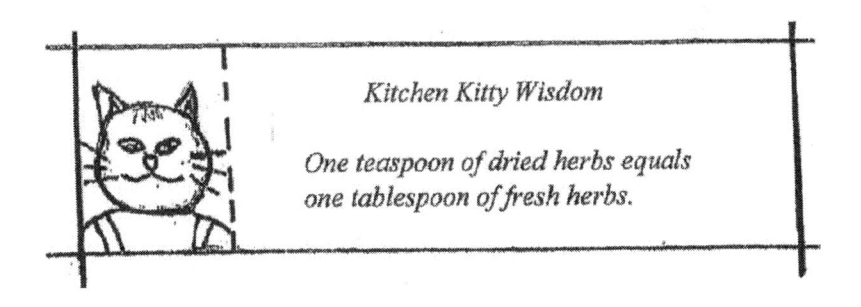

Kitchen Kitty Wisdom

One teaspoon of dried herbs equals one tablespoon of fresh herbs.

About the Editors

Rita E. Westphal (R. E. Westphal) holds a BA degree in English Education and Business Administration and is retired from a career in supervisory management. She is currently an active community volunteer. She enjoys cooking, quilting, nature walks and is an avid genealogy enthusiast. She is a published author of a short story and several poems. Reach her at az.sfu2019@outlook.com .

Mary Jo Stumreiter Nickum was born on November 6, 1945 in Richmond, Indiana to Mary and Joe Stumreiter. As an infant she moved with her parents to Fifield, Wisconsin. Joe and Mary bought a farm with a substantial woodlot where Mary Jo and her sister were raised.

Mary Jo attended St. Anthony's Catholic elementary school and graduated from Park Falls (Lincoln) High School. She went on to earn a B. A. degree in English education. From there she earned an M. Lib. in library science from the University of Washington and later, earned a Master's in Interdisciplinary Studies (M A.I.S.) from Oregon State University. She continued her work as a professional librarian until she took medical retirement because of her worsening multiple sclerosis (MS) in 1994.

Made in the USA
San Bernardino, CA
29 June 2019